UNIVERSITY OF
WOLVERHAMPTON
KNOWLEDGE • INNOVATION • ENTERPRISE

Harrison Learning Centre
City Campus
University of Wolverhampton
St Peter's Square
Wolverhampton WV1 1RH
Telephone: 0845 408 1631
Online Renewals:
www.wlv.ac.uk/lib/myaccount

Telephone Renewals: 01902 321333 or 0845 408 1631
Online Renewals: www.wlv.ac.uk/lib/myaccount
Please return this item on or before the last date shown above.
Fines will be charged if items are returned late.

See tariff of fines displayed at the Counter.   (L2)

People, Groups and Society

Hedy Brown

Open University Press

Milton Keynes · Philadelphia

Open University Press
Open University Educational Enterprises Limited
12 Cofferidge Close
Stony Stratford
Milton Keynes MK11 1BY, England

and
242 Cherry Street
Philadelphia, PA 19106, USA

First Published 1985

British Library Cataloguing in Publication Data

Brown, Hedy
  People, groups, and society.
  1. Social groups
  I. Title
  302.3   HM131

  ISBN 0-335-15140-X
  ISBN 0-335-15139-6 Pbk

Library of Congress Cataloging in Publication Data

Brown, Hedy.
  People, groups, and society.

  Bibliography: p.
  Includes index.
  1. Social groups.   2. Social interaction.   3. Social
control.   4. Crowds.   I. Title.
  HM131.B72   1985   302.3   85-11599

  ISBN 0-335-15140-X
  ISBN 0-335-15139-6 (Pbk)

Text design by Nicola Sheldon
Typeset by Colset Private Limited, Singapore
Printed in Great Britain at the Alden Press, Oxford

Contents

Preface

I would like to acknowledge that this book has benefited from the stimulation and creative tension of working with my colleagues at the Open University.

I would like to thank Jeannette Murphy of the Polytechnic of North London for commenting on an early draft of this book. Any shortcomings of the text which remain are of course entirely mine.

I would also like to thank Ortenz Opheelia Rose for sustained secretarial support.

Hedy Brown
March, 1985

Introduction

Much of our time is spent in relationships with other people — at work or leisure, at home or in a public place. It is not surprising then that the study of such relationships and encounters has been a long-standing interest of social scientists — psychiatrists, anthropologists, sociologists and others — and that it has also captured the imagination and concern of social philosophers and the public at large.

This book approaches the exploration of social interactions from a social psychological perspective and its primary focus is on the study of *groups*, the processes operating within groups and the effects of group membership on the participants. However, as the title of this book implies, groups and group membership need to be considered with reference both to people (the attitudes, expectations or past experience of group members) and the societal context (such as the prevailing climate of opinion or the wider social structure within which the group operates). One key question which has fascinated social psychologists is the extent to which individuals are influenced by their social partners in the group and the extent to which they retain their independence of thought and action. Not only is this a question of considerable interest in its own right — and a question which will be confronted right through this book — but the insights gained from studying the way people relate to others can be and have been used to attempt to exert influence on people and control them. The study of groups is therefore also of interest to the politician, social worker, teacher and others concerned to influence and change people. Group membership, as we shall see in this book, can be constraining, indeed damaging to people or, in other circumstances, it can be supportive of the individual and help him or her withstand pressures from outside the group. In addition, a good case can be made for stating that the *small* group has a particular importance in human life. This view is based on the recognition that at birth the human infant is dependent for survival on the care given to him or her by other people and that, in consequence, some form of biological family or other kind of caretaking group is necessary and indeed universal in human society. Given the initial helplessness of the new-born child it is not surprising that it has been found that the infant is born with attributes such as a predisposition to respond to the human face which mark him or her as a *social* being. This need for, and capacity to respond to, other people, whether thought of as innate or learned in the early interactions with the child's caretakers, may well form a life-long human attribute and constitute the basic reason why people spontaneously seek out others (even where there is no 'objective' reason for their being together as when a task needs their cooperation). It is because of this that Cooley pointed out as early as 1902 that small spontaneously formed groups rather than single individuals should be thought of as the 'natural' human entity. It follows that it is the outcast, hermit or 'loner' who are deviants though they can survive, in some sort of fashion, outside human companionship since they already carry in their minds a symbolic representation of their social world which informs and constructs their behaviour and experience. They are also likely to have learned such skills as they need for survival before entering a voluntary or enforced state of isolation. Equally, 'feral' children, that is those allegedly reared by wolves or other wild animals, must initially have had some human care to survive. As we shall see, research and theorizing about groups goes far beyond the small 'primary' group but it is as well to point out at the outset that it is reasonable to assume that it is part of 'human nature' to form associations with other people.

The word 'group' has been applied to many entities — small or large groups, informal or formal groups, groups which have a short life (for instance those set up in a laboratory for the duration of a brief experiment) or those which have a long-term existence. Groups also differ in their functions, purposes, goals, in their history and in the wider social contexts in which they occur. I shall not, therefore, provide a definition of 'groups' here at the beginning of this book as such a definition would either have to be bland (and, therefore, virtually without meaning) or it would prejudge the questions we shall explore. Hence we will examine definitions of the concept of group as we consider empirical research and the theoretical traditions which have given rise to such work.

One other point ought to be emphasized at the beginning. It concerns the level of analysis at which the researcher, theorist or practitioner operates. Social scientists usually identify three levels of analysis — the individual, the group and the wider society, its structure or culture. These levels can be treated as distinct though we shall see that there are multidirectional influences between individuals, groups and society. Individuals can adopt, reject or modify the wider society's values and standards and group membership can be an important context and catalyst in which these psychological processes take place.

In research on groups most frequently the dependent variable, that is that which is measured as the outcome, is the *group's effect on individuals* (in terms of modifications to their perceptions, judgements, decisions, opinions or behaviour). However, the locus of explanation (the independent variable) can be conceived as being on a variety of levels of analysis and it is important to be clear in one's own mind as to the level at which one operates. Thus one may focus on factors which are attributes of *individuals* — their attitudes, values, personality traits; the 'fit' of their attitudes with those of others in the group; their need for acceptance by other people, in general, or by members of a particular group. All these may affect how people perceive group expectations or pressures and how they respond to them.

Researchers and theorists can also operate at the level of analysis of the *group*, taking the properties of the group as their independent variables. Hence social psychologists have studied the social structure of groups, such as the pattern of communication which has sprung up informally among members or which follows from the organizational structure of a firm or which has been imposed by the experimenter in the laboratory. The explanations on this level of analysis are no longer in terms of the attributes of the individuals comprising the group but in terms of the characteristics of the group which give rise to social interactions (which, it is assumed, would be of a different kind if the characteristics of the group were different). These, in turn, affect the individual members of the group.

There is a further level of analysis, the *societal level*, which needs to be considered. Social interactions occur among individuals whose relative status, authority or power neither derive (wholly) from their own characteristics nor (wholly) from their position or roles in the group but (partly, though again not wholly) from the social context *beyond* the immediate group which is being studied. For instance, a teacher's influence may be determined not only by his or her personality, knowledge, teaching style and the match or mismatch between those attributes and the children's expectations but by the status, authority or power inherent in a teacher's *role* (and the place of that role in the social structure). The attributes of such roles derive from the attitudes, values or ideologies prevalent in a given society. To account fully for the teacher's influence (or lack of it), we will therefore also need to study the teacher — pupils group from a *societal, cultural* and, indeed, *historical perspective* (since attitudes to authority or to the importance of schooling may change over a period of time or be different in different societies). Explanations on this level of analysis are in terms of the social positions or social categorizations of the individuals involved. These explanations refer to factors beyond the immediate group though, again, the evidence for their relevance and influence within the group will have to be noted in the changes they bring about (or to which they contribute) in individuals.

Much of the research on groups has focused on intra-individual or intragroup factors and has neglected this societal level of analysis. It is, however, specifically considered when the interaction *between* groups is studied.

The notion of levels of analysis is important not only in research strategies and in the identification of the underlying causes of an event, behaviour or experience but in terms of the search for remedies or improvements to a problem. For example, if we wish to change people's attitudes to, and perceptions of, racial minorities or the unemployed, we need to consider whether it would be more appropriate to influence people *directly* through persuasion and other psychological means (whether individually or in groups) or *indirectly* through changing the social context, for instance, by legislation; alternatively we may try to initiate change on all these levels.

This book, in presenting the research and theories of social psychologists in studying *people, groups and society* also considers the scientific, ethical and practical problems they have faced in their pursuit. Their work is continuing and, at times, gives rise to as many questions and paradoxes as answers. Readers of this book should therefore think of themselves as undertaking a voyage of discovery, noting the difficulties and delights of doing social psychology as well as reflecting on the relevance of social psychology to themselves as *social* human beings. The latter should not be too difficult since social psychologists tend to focus on issues which are seen by them (and by other members of their society) as giving rise to concern — issues such as conformity, authoritarianism, propaganda, race relations, crowd behaviour, 'brainwashing', pressure groups and many other topics, all of which consider people in the context of their group membership and their wider society. Given the immediacy of these issues, the reader is provided with real world examples and can relate his or her experience to the research discussed. Such a preoccupation with topics of current concern, however, poses its own difficulties and is sometimes seen as an obstacle to the development of a truly scientific academic discipline. Thus, if the questions one asks stem from contemporary contexts, then the answers one obtains may be of validity only in these same contexts. Both questions and answers may need revision in the light of changing social conditions. Whilst, therefore, research findings and their meaning and implications need to be assessed with caution, the spur to much social psychological research in the first place has been the optimistic view that the knowledge gained from research will enable social psychologists (or those in a position to act on their findings) to introduce changes in society with beneficial outcomes for that society and its members. However, such interventions may be undertaken on the basis of what may turn out to be insufficient evidence and may cause unforeseen effects or raise unforeseen ethical issues.

These difficulties and challenges are implicit in social psychology as a whole but will be explored in this volume specifically in considering research and theories relating to the effects of groups on their members and the relevance and implications of such research for everyday life. Hence the focus of this book is on two interlaced strands:

(a) the influence of the wider social context and what appears as 'problematic' in society (and hence the selection of *topics* or *issues* for research); and
(b) developments and progress within the discipline (and hence *how* phenomena are studied and explained).

These two traditions of research — 'applied' and 'pure' — also broadly reflect differences in methodology. Thus the applied social psychologist tends to engage in field research and the pure theoretician of group processes, concerned not with social issues but with the advance of science, tends to use laboratory experiments. However, you will find that these distinctions have become somewhat blurred, certainly in the study of groups, and that many important issues have been researched by both the theoretician and the applied researcher, through field experiments and observation as well as through laboratory based experiments. Equally, the applied researcher can hope to contribute to theory and the pure researcher may be able to extend our understanding of the processes at work in a 'real-life' issue. Indeed, one and the same person can take a problem into the laboratory and, at another time, study it in a more realistic context.

In Section I of this book we will discuss some key studies, ranging from the 1930s to the present day, which will illustrate the methods and findings and changing concerns of social psychologists when studying groups.

In Section II we will explore how this knowledge has been used deliberately to influence people's convictions and behaviour and our discussion will range from persuasion to 'brainwashing'.

In Section III we will turn to the study of intergroup relations and there such topics as prejudice, stereotyping, the causes of intergroup conflict and their possible resolution will be considered.

In Section IV we will explore whether 'crowds' differ from 'groups' and whether crowd phenomena can be explained through concepts and theories which have been evolved in the study of groups.

Section V will pick up some loose ends and offer some reflections on what to conclude from the earlier parts of the book.

SECTION I

Group Membership and Social Influence: From Conformity to Innovation

As has been pointed out in the Introduction, social psychologists explore issues which are considered as 'problems' in their own societies; at the same time they are also concerned to study them as scientifically as possible and to develop theories which would account for their findings. In the first section, we shall consider a number of studies which will illustrate these two concerns. In addition, these studies will begin to provide us with a vocabulary, both descriptive and explanatory, with which to discuss group phenomena and it will begin to introduce the range of research methods used by social psychologists. Chronologically, this section ranges from the 1930s to the present day and the studies we will consider illustrate changing foci of research as well as developments in social psychological theory. The early examples of research (from the 1930s and 1940s), inspite of these developments, are still crucial benchmarks in social psychology.

Social psychologists in the 1930s were much concerned at the apparent ease with which European dictators of that period managed to influence their own nationals and gain ascendancy over public opinion and behaviour. These preoccupations led to two foci of research. One explored the extent of the influence of the mass media and we will consider some of these findings in Section II. Here we will review the work of those social psychologists who tried to understand the influence processes at work *within* groups and the effect of group membership on individuals.

The formation of and adherence to social norms

Social norms, that is generally accepted ways of behaving, are learnt during childhood and right through life, from experience or explicit instruction. Such norms enable people to interact effectively with each other, as each individual in a social exchange knows what to expect from other people and how to act towards them appropriately (that is, in ways which they, in turn, will understand, find acceptable and to which they can respond).

Much confusion can be caused when people from two cultures meet who have different norms of behaviour. An Englishman might be put off by a Frenchman greeting him by kissing him on both cheeks or an Englishwoman might cause consternation in another society by smoking in public or conversing freely with men. But not all interactions are governed by such generally accepted cultural norms. Many social encounters give rise to their own norms and rules of behaviour. In fact, this is such a common phenomenon that the term 'external norms' is used to refer to broad societal norms and the term 'internal norms' is applied to those norms which arise during the interactions of people in a particular group. The first series of studies I want to consider was carried out by Sherif in the 1930s. His experiments provide striking evidence for the formation of such internal norms. The situations he used were unusual in that those participating in the experiment could not fall back on previous experience, values or frames of reference as a guide to their own actions. What, then, did Sherif do? [see Box 1]

[handwritten annotation: nut - 1 person out room. Agrees with others so as not to be different]

Box 1 The formation of norms (Sherif, 1936).

Sherif seated his male subjects, initially one at a time, in a completely dark room in which the experimenter exposed a point of light for a few seconds. This point of light *remains stationary but appears to move*. This is an optical illusion known as the 'autokinetic effect'. The subjects were asked to estimate aloud how far the light had moved in each of one hundred exposures. Wide variations were found in the judgements made by different individuals but each subjectively established a distinct range of estimates, peculiar to himself, and a characteristic personal 'norm' (the figure he called out most frequently), the result of basing later estimates on those made earlier. In other words, he established for himself a frame of reference in a situation where he lacked objective criteria because he found himself in literal and figurative darkness. When each individual was put into the same experimental situation again on subsequent days it was found that each tended to preserve his newly developed personal 'response norm' but made his estimates within a narrower range.

Sherif next turned to explore the reactions of individuals in two- or three-person groups. Would individuals again evolve their idiosyncratic frames of reference or would they act together in establishing a range, and a reference point within that range, peculiar to the *group*?

Sherif used two types of group situations. He studied the reactions of individuals who were put into the group situation first and only subsequently experienced the stimulus situation on their own. The reactions of these subjects were compared to those who first faced the stimulus situation alone and subsequently went through the experiment in groups of two or three. In all these situations, the subjects were instructed to give their *own* judgements and the post-experimental interviews confirm that they did not think of themselves as members of a group in which they would jointly arrive at agreed judgements. Nevertheless, whilst merely making their estimates in each other's presence what can only be called a *group norm* emerged — quickly when subjects had not previously experienced this situation and a little more slowly when subjects had previously evolved individual ranges and norms (see Figure 1A and 1B). When individuals who had first experienced the situation together with other subjects subsequently faced the same situation alone they perceived it in terms of the range and norms they brought to it from the group situation.

What conclusions can we draw from Sherif's findings and do they, based as they were on a contrived situation, contribute to our understanding of the world outside the laboratory?

First, these results demonstrate that the subjects in these experiments tend to structure unstructured situations in that they establish for themselves a frame of reference within which they act with some confidence; in other words, *they impose a structure on a meaningless situation* and thus imbue it with meaning.

Secondly, these results demonstrate that subjects do not passively record what is going on around them but that the frames of reference which they develop in a situation, or which they bring to it, *modify the perception* of the stimuli to which they are exposed.

Thirdly, and this is what we are concerned with here, these results suggest that subjects *adjust their judgements to bring them into line with those of other people* even when they do not think of themselves as engaged in a common endeavour. We may infer that, at any rate in our culture, to be in accord with other people satisfies an important psychological need, particularly in situations where people lack certainty or the possibility of validating their own opinions other than by a comparison with those held by others. Through such 'social comparison' processes (Festinger, 1954) a common social reality is established and validated.

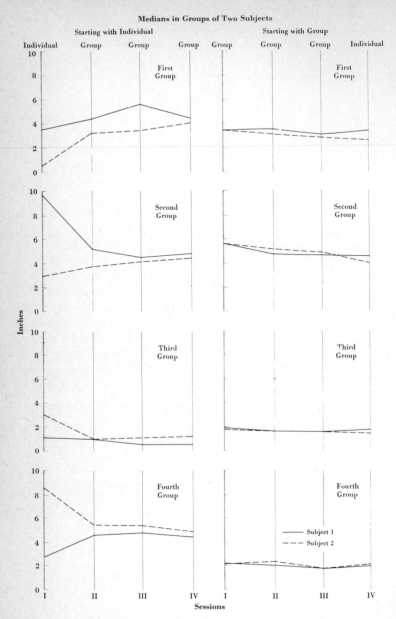

FIGURE 1A.   Medians in groups of two subjects

*The graphs on the left in Figures 1A and 1B illustrate
the formation of group norms, where the individual has first evolved
his own norms in estimating the distance the light moves.
The graph on the right in Figures 1A and 1B illustrate that group
norms are retained when the individual estimates distances on his own.*

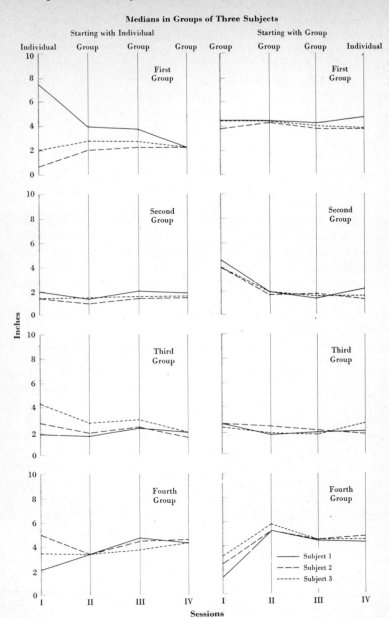

Medians in Groups of Three Subjects

FIGURE 1B. Medians in groups of three subjects

SOURCE: Sherif, M. (1936) The Psychology of Social Norms, New York, Harper and Row.

Whilst Sherif's experiments (and later replications) almost invariably demonstrate this *convergence* of estimates among subjects in two or three-person groups, post-experimental interviews reveal that the subjects themselves are unaware of being influenced. Indeed they hotly deny being affected by the estimates made by others in the group. It is interesting to speculate whether such subjects would have managed to evolve their own norms and range of estimates and stick to them if they had been told that a prize would go to the individual who made the 'best' estimates. We do not know since such an experiment is not recorded, but, given that the subjects were unaware of being influenced by others during these sessions, one might expect that they could not guard against such influences, whatever their motivation.

The essence of a laboratory experiment is the experimenter's ability to vary one aspect whilst all other conditions remain the same and, as a consequence, one may reasonably attribute the outcome to the particular change which was introduced into the situation. Thus Sherif demonstrated that an individual on his own will show different reactions to the same stimulus as compared to when he is with others. Nevertheless, other aspects may 'intrude' from outside the experimental situation. Frequently, as we shall see, individual differences or prior attitudes and values or the wider social context may affect the extent to which the independent variable has an effect. The results of psychological experiments, therefore, are not as unequivocal as they may at first appear. There is always a need for careful interpretation or even speculation. I make these points here because they apply to a study reported by Sherif and Sherif (1969). This study was based on the autokinetic effect and took place in a monastery. Here, conflict ensued between the monks and novices who were subjects in the same session and *no convergence of estimates took place*. This study (though such explanations were not used at the time) may well illustrate the point I made in the Introduction concerning the need to take societal factors into account. Though one would expect the novices to agree with the monks (if only so as not to fall prey to the sin of pride) the tensions between them or perhaps their perceptions of difference in their roles and status, 'intruded' into the experimental situation, though it was an artificial situation which depended upon an optical illusion and was apparently divorced from any real life event or concern.

Sherif's experiments are important because their significance extends beyond the perception of an optical illusion; they mirror what we can see going on all around us, namely, that the expectations, attitudes and values of people influence their perception of and reaction to stimuli in their environment. Think, for instance, of your work situation. Could you understand your reaction to a change in work schedules, method of payment, the leadership style of the supervisor or anything else without reference both to your own previous experience and to the values, attitudes and expectations of the people around you? And these, in turn, will have resulted from *their* experience as members of the present work group and/or of other groups such as their union, family, social class and so on.

Sherif's work focused on a small group. Outside the laboratory, such groups have often been referred to as *primary groups* because of their importance to the individual. Primary groups are always small groups in which all members have face-to-face contacts. The relationships of people in such groups are therefore close and often intimate. Families, play groups, work or sport teams are examples of such groupings.

Small primary groups can be *informal*, that is, they can arise spontaneously such as when children living in the same street congregate together and form a gang. Primary groups, however, can also be *formal*, such as a work team brought together by management to accomplish a given task. In formal groups some of the important goals and roles of members ar predetermined: for instance the expected standards of production, adherence to safety rules or behaviour towards colleagues are already laid down when a newcomer joins the firm. In informal groupings, on the other hand, goals, roles, attitudes and norms of behaviour tend to arise out of the current interactions of the group members. However, once established, adherence to such internal norms by individuals may indicate to others that they consider themselves, and wish to be considered by others, members of this group. The extent to which members uphold the group's norms is taken as an indication of the *cohesiveness* of the group.

Formally constituted groups, such as work teams, in which some of the norms, rules and goals for their members' behaviour have been established prior to their recruitment and interaction with each other, also evolve *informal* or internal norms and forms of behaviour. Some of these may interfere with the formal or external norms and demands of the organization. For instance, incentive schemes may be ignored by group members informally agreeing to restrict their output (as was demonstrated in the famous Hawthorne studies (Roethlisberger and Dickson, 1939)).

The norms evolved in the primary group are often the ones which govern the individual's behaviour whether or not such norms are in accordance with those of the larger *secondary groups* of which the smaller primary groups may be a part. (The term *secondary groups* has been used by social psychologists to describe larger and usually formally constituted entities such as factories, schools, political parties or clubs).

There are several reasons why people may be more likely to adhere to the standards and expectations of their immediate primary groups. For one thing, these standards and expectations can be readily perceived within the primary group. For another, conformity to group norms brings psychological rewards through the acceptance by and support of other members — that is, if we assume that there is a deeply felt need in human beings for attention or a response from others, whether such a need is innate or has evolved from childhood experience of dependence and attachment to caretakers. A further reason for adherence to the norms of members of one's immediate primary groups is based on the capacity of group members to exert pressure on deviants through withdrawal of affection, verbal admonitions or abuse and ridicule, physical assault, exclusion from the group (such as 'sending a member to Coventry') or 'blacking' someone's work. Such pressures may be directed towards a person's *behaviour* rather than his or her *attitudes* since behaviour is visible whilst attitudes can be kept private. How far norms are upheld by members (in other words, how cohesive the group is) depends on the *meaning* which the group has for them, the opportunities they have of joining other groups and the reasons for joining a particular group in the first place. An individual is likely to want to balance the *psychological cost* of changing behaviour or opinions to conform to the group with the *psychological reward* of being liked and accepted by others in the group.

Membership and reference groups

In the last section we explored the formation of norms in the context of a series of laboratory experiments. In this section I want to review another study carried out in the 1930s in which Newcomb (1952) studied the changing attitudes of students towards public issues, not in the laboratory but in the 'real-life' situation of a residential college. Such a study, from a methodological point of view, is a field study. This study, too, continues to interest social psychologists, first because in analysing the findings it uses the concepts *membership groups* and *reference groups* which are still part of our current social psychological vocabulary, and secondly, because further insights were gained when the students were surveyed again twenty-five years later.

The term membership group simply refers to a group of which people are members by virtue of their presence in it. By contrast, the term reference group, first used by Hyman (1942), refers to groups with which individuals compare themselves in evaluating their status. The concept, however, became part of social-psychological terminology through its use by Newcomb (Newcomb, 1952) in discussing his findings concerning attitude change among the students at Bennington College, outlined in Box 2.

Box 2   Membership and reference groups in a college for women students (Newcomb, 1952).

Bennington was (and is) an expensive East Coast American residential university college for women students. At the time at which the study was carried out (in the 1930s) most of its students came from wealthy conservative families. On arrival at the college these girls on the whole held conservative political views, that is, they had a pre-existing set of norms, but during their four-year stay at Bennington they were exposed to the more liberal (radical) attitudes of the teaching staff and senior students. There was a deliberate emphasis in the college on the discussion of a wide range of social problems, partly because this was a time of many stresses (the Depression) and attempts at social change (the New Deal), and partly because the teaching staff felt that, quite apart from any academic subject that students might study, they should become acquainted with the problems of their contemporary world.

As a result of these policies and attitudes of the staff, most of the girls underwent a marked shift in their attitudes, from relatively conservative to relatively liberal views, over the four years of their stay in the college. This is perhaps what one might expect in a fairly closely-knit, relatively small community (250 students) with an active liberal leadership. However, since not *all* the students changed their views in the expected direction, the effect cannot be attributed simply to the physical presence of a person in the group. In other words, the fact that Bennington College is a girl's *membership group* does not in itself explain the shift in opinion towards the 'prestige' attitudes in the college. The crucial variable appears to be whether or not the student adopts the college community as a *positive reference group* for her own political attitudes. Interviews revealed that those girls who took the community as a *negative reference group* (that is, they felt hostile to it), and the home and family as a positive reference group for their political attitudes, remained unaffected by the liberal ethos of the college and continued to be conservative. They tended to have only a few friends at college. For some, the college was a positive reference group as a social focus but not a positive point of reference for political attitudes (and these girls, too, did not change their outlook but they did make many friends). Among those whose attitudes did change, the college was a positive reference group for political views and, in addition, for these students, their parents may or may not have come to be viewed as a negative reference group: that is, some students took the college community as a reference point for their political attitudes without necessarily distancing themselves from their parents.

Why some of the students continued to take their home and family as a positive point of reference, whilst others took their new membership group as a positive point of reference, is a separate question and was not explored by Newcomb. The terms 'membership group' and 'reference group' are basically descriptive rather than explanatory concepts. Essentially, those who remained unaffected by the majority views in the college either had well thought-out conservative opinions (as opposed to merely 'complying' with parental views) or they were, in Newcomb's rather value-laden estimation, 'over-dependent' on home and parents. In a few cases they simply had other interests and made neither their home and family nor the college a point of reference for their attitudes.

The vast majority of the students did alter their political outlook and Newcomb thought that *in a different group they might have changed in a different way*. He concluded that attitudes are not acquired in a social vacuum and that attitudinal change is a function of how an individual relates to the total membership group and to one or more reference groups. The probability of change also depends on the strength of the initial attitude and the discrepancy between one's own attitudinal position and that of people in one's new membership group. Furthermore, in 'yielding' to perceived group expectations, personality differences may play a part.

Newcomb, nevertheless, concluded — from the fact that most girls did adopt increasingly liberal views and on the basis of psychiatric interviews — that *it is 'normal' to make one's current membership group one's (positive) reference group*.

Some twenty-five years later Newcomb et al. (1967) carried out a follow-up study. He found that very few of the women he contacted had reverted to the conservative attitudes which they held before they attended Bennington College. Both the women (and their husbands) tended to have markedly more liberal views than a comparable sample of American women of the *same* socio-economic level. These findings can be accounted for in three ways:

(a) the values adopted during their stay at Bennington were 'internalized' (Kelman, 1958);
(b) the four years spent at Bennington proved such a satisfying experience that the College remained a vital reference group and focus in their lives; and/or
(c) the persistence of liberal views was a function of later liberal associations — husbands and friends — who were themselves chosen partly because of these shared beliefs.

Although the distinction between 'membership' and 'reference' group is descriptive rather than explanatory, thinking about group membership in those terms may lead to further insights. For instance, a man may be a plumber and hence described as working class. He however, may think of himself as a middle-class businessman and, perhaps, express his class membership by voting Conservative. *Why* he does this requires further elucidation, but recognizing that 'objective' indices of occupation and class membership do not necessarily indicate a person's reference groups (and the self-image he or she has) is a useful beginning.

Are the findings obtained by Sherif and Newcomb compatible? At first sight the *contrast* between their studies seems most marked. Sherif's groups are artificial; the subjects do not have norms about the situation into which they are plunged; they form temporary groups; the groups are face-to-face. Newcomb's groups are real groups; the subjects have norms (political attitudes) which are relevant to their situation; the groups are relatively long-term; and two kinds of groups are considered; membership and reference groups (and the same group may be both a reference and a membership group but not invariably so).

The conclusions of both authors, however, are *compatible* and *similar*: they both stress the *importance of group membership*, Sherif to the formation and maintenance of norms, Newcomb to the change of attitudes. Newcomb further stresses that one's membership group (which can be large or small) tends to become one's reference group.

Group pressure

The studies we have already reviewed testify to the power of group membership in forming or changing the norms or attitudes of people. In both Sherif's and Newcomb's studies interviews with subjects revealed that they experienced doubts or felt under pressure, but their subjective experience was not the main focus of the research.

Another series of classic and influential studies carried out by S.E. Asch in the 1940s, however, did focus on the psychological pressures experienced by an individual or a small minority who disagree with the opinions or judgements expressed by the majority. Asch's immediate objective was to study the conditions which induce individuals either to resist group pressures or to yield to them, even when the views expressed by the majority are perceived by the subjects to be *contrary to fact*. See Box 3.

Box 3   Asch's experiment on group pressure (Asch, 1952).

Asch asked a group of male subjects to judge which of three lines presented on a card matched a standard comparison line on another card. In each group there were seven 'confederates' of the experimenter (also called 'stooges') and one 'naive' subject, that is, a 'real' subject who did not know that the other people present had specific instructions as to how to act. The naive subject was always seated so as to be the second last person to call out his judgement. (If he had been last, the manipulation might have been too obvious.) Initially, the seven 'stooges' named the same (correct) line and so, of course, did the naive member of the group. But then the experimenter's confederates began to make incorrect judgements about which line matched the standard line and thus the true subject was faced with a conflict between the judgements expressed by the other group members (who had established their credibility in his eyes through their earlier correct judgements) and the information coming to him from his own senses. In the baseline experiment it was quite obvious which of the lines was the matching line — see Figure 2. Subjects experienced bewilderment, tension and stress, but (and this is the question in which Asch was interested) did they yield to the majority's opinion or did they stick to their own judgements? In the basic condition, described above, in about one third of the judgements the subject changed his response and answered in accordance with the group's false judgements. To put this another way, two thirds of all the judgements were given without yielding to group pressure. However, there were great *individual differences*: one in four people never conformed, whilst others virtually always came to agree with the group. Post-experimental interviews revealed that the 'independent' subjects frequently experienced conflict or tension and doubt but they were resilient in shaking off oppressive group pressures. Others were able to isolate themselves mentally from the group and hence were also able to maintain their individuality. Post-experimental interviews also suggested that some of the 'yielding' subjects unconsciously distorted their perceptions — they actually 'saw' the lines in the way the stooges said they did. Most though, although they still saw the lines correctly, thought they must be misperceiving them and distorted their *judgements* to fit in with the group. A third category of yielders did not misperceive the lines, nor did they conclude that the majority was right; they yielded because of an overpowering need not to appear different from others.

Asch's experiments show that there are individual differences which lead some people to yield and others to remain independent (and you may well speculate on how you would have reacted!). The actual conditions of the experiment, however, also influence the outcome. Thus, in later experiments the difficulty of the task was increased by making the differences between the lines smaller. In this more ambiguous and confusing condition more subjects conformed to the group's judgements. When a subject was joined by another genuine subject, however, resistance to the views expressed by the other members of the group increased even though the two were still only a *minority* in the group. (Much later, the study of how minorities achieve influence became a flourishing research topic;

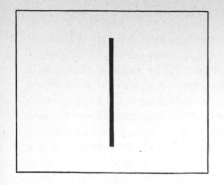 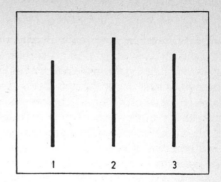

FIGURE 2.   *Subjects were shown a series of two cards, one with always the same standard line, the other with three lines of varying lengths, one of which matched the standard line. Subjects were asked to indicate which of the three lines was the matching line. Below is an example of the two cards shown.*

SOURCE: Asch, S.E. (1955) 'Opinions and social pressure', *Scientific American*, November.

these studies will be discussed on pages 30—38). We may conclude from this series of experiments that whether individuals use the judgements made by members of their group for comparison purposes where they cannot independently verify their own impressions (for example, by measuring the lines) and whether they yield to them or resist them in making their own judgements, depends on several things:

(a) the characteristics of the stimulus, in this case how clear the differences are between the lines; more generally, the nature of social reality or the task;

(b) the group structure, in this case whether the subject is the only apparent deviant;

(c) individual differences; and,

(d) as we shall see in a moment, the cultural expectations of conformity subjects bring to the experiment from their contemporary world.

Asch's experiments were widely replicated, usually with American college students as subjects. The results were fairly consistent and accord with the original findings though there were significant differences when people in a number of countries were tested. For instance, when Milgram (1961) compared Norwegian and French students carrying out this experiment, it was the Norwegian students who more readily agreed with the majority. Milgram speculated that Norwegians form a more homogenous and cohesive group than do the French and that they are therefore less tolerant of differences that may threaten cohesiveness. More interesting, perhaps, is a study by Larsen (1974) several decades after the original work which demonstrated significantly lower rates of conformity in American students than Asch had found. Larsen attributes this to the changed climate of opinion in America in the 1970s which encouraged independence and criticism rather than conformity. Even more recently Perrin and Spencer (1981) found in a British study that in only one out of 396 trials did a subject join the erroneous majority though, like Asch's subjects, they experienced tension and stress. It must be pointed out, however, that their subjects were engineering, mathematics and chemistry students, well able to judge the length of lines and therefore in a strong position to resist psychological pressures to agree with inaccurate judgements on this particular task. I will come back to this point (that knowledge is a safeguard against pressures to conform) later on in this Section. Perrin and Spencer in the same paper also report rates of conformity approaching those of Asch when their subjects were young offenders on probation, the majority in the group were probation officers and the experimenter was an 'authority figure'. This does suggest that their and Larsen's *student* subjects (unlike the young offenders) were less in awe of their experimenters than were Asch's original ones (they called him 'sir' in interviews!) and that is, indeed, part of the cultural differences we are concerned with. People in the 1960s and early 1970s may have been more independent, questioning, critical or, perhaps, more knowledgeable about psychology (and hence more sceptical) than those in the 1950s and it is these characteristics which affect how they behave in the course of an experiment.

Larsen (1982) makes the point that a later study by him and his colleagues (Larsen *et al.*, 1979) showed a return by the late 1970s to the levels of conformity found in the Asch situation in the 1950s. He explains this by speculating that the American students of the late 1970s were again returning to the concerns of students in the 1950s and were more involved in preparation for jobs and careers than were their predecessors in the 1974 study who were motivated by social concerns and manifested lower rates of conformity.

Larsen claims that the results suggest a relationship between broader social changes and laboratory conformity in that in the United States during the 1950s (the period of McCarthyism) students exhibited high conformity, whilst the more questioning students of the Vietnam War era produced low conformity and students in the later 1970s again produced high conformity. Larsen further points out that during the last decade many students (by contrast with the 1960s 'activist' generation) joined mystical movements and religions which would also suggest less concern with independence and individuality. (We will return to this point again when discussing membership of sects on pages 88–91.)

Nicholson *et al.* (1985) in studying the 'Asch effect' in British and American student populations found that 'although the degree of conformity to a unanimous peer group opinion is far less than that reported 30 years ago, it remains *observable* in university students in both Britain and the US.' Their results on student populations therefore differ from those of Perrin and Spencer (1981). I have already pointed out that the latter authors had a very specially qualified sample of subjects. However, Nicholson *et al.* (1985) who had gathered their data on British students in May 1983 speculate that the 'Falkland factor' had led to an increase in British cohesiveness (and hence to a greater response to group pressure). They suggest that the 'Asch paradigm may provide a useful indicator of fluctuations in group cohesion over time and in changing national circumstances'.

The results of such replications of Asch's experiment in different social climates illustrate the point I made earlier that social psychologists need to be aware of and take into account the 'societal level' of analysis even when studying intra-group or individual phenomena.

Discrepancies in experimental outcomes may also illustrate that it is not only the subjects who have changed their attitudes in a changed climate of opinion but the experimenters, too, may have been affected and may no longer expect conformity to be demonstrated to the extent it was in Asch's original study. Hence, even when Asch's paradigm is apparently faithfully replicated, the experimenter may, unwittingly, convey to the subjects certain expectations as to the outcome of the experiment. Such unintended 'experimenter effects' are quite common and may present difficulties in interpreting the results of experiments. This has been documented by Orne (1962) and Rosenthal (1966).

The fact that the 'Zeitgeist' (literally the spirit of the time, that is, the prevailing political or social mood of the period) may affect the outcomes of experiments raises questions about the status of psychological research. If the same experiment can produce different results in different historical periods, are we to conclude that there are no universal truths in social psychology? Are findings, whether derived from experiments or field research, only valid in the context of the place and time where they were undertaken? The answer to both these questions is a qualified 'yes' in many areas of *social* psychology. However, the fact that social psychologists may not be dealing with universal truths does not make social psychological research either unimportant or uninteresting. The findings of social psychology help us understand our own times and, where a topic has been studied over a period of time, they also document the changes which have taken place in society and in the expectations and attitudes of people. Indeed, I would argue that far from being a drawback it is an advantage of social psychology that its practitioners are engaged in illuminating for us our contemporary world. Furthermore, where, for instance, we are trying to understand the *nature* of the psychological processes through which an individual is influenced, we may still arrive at valid and possibly long-lasting insights even though the *extent* to which such processes operate may vary from one historical period or one society to another and, indeed, from one individual to another.

Obedience to authority

Words such as conformity or compliance are concepts used in everyday life and they denote 'acceptance of influence'. Psychologists, as we have already seen, also use these terms and they have over a period of time endeavoured to define them more precisely, indeed to distinguish between them and to analyse the psychological processes which give rise to them. I will come back to these issues on pages 21—30.

At this point it is useful to review another series of psychological experiments in which a further term denoting 'acceptance of influence' was used. The studies were carried out by Milgram between 1960 and 1963 and later brought together in a book (Milgram, 1974). Milgram used the phrase *obedience to authority* to explain what he observed in his research. He argues that there is a difference between obedience and conformity though he sees both as involving the abdication of personal responsibility. He views conformity as going along with one's peers in a group, whilst obedience is accorded to a person of authority in a hierarchical situation. Influence of one person over another, then, in this view arises from social power and status rather than from a psychological 'need' for acceptance by others. People usually deny that they conform (because of the value judgements attaching to this word) but they may be quite willing to make excuses for themselves by saying they *obeyed orders*.

Milgram considers obedience a basic element of social life and a determinant of behaviour of particular relevance to our time. His interest in obedience stems from the fact that millions of people were murdered in concentration camps during the Second World War, not necessarily by particularly evil men and women but through the operation of a bureaucratic process which depended on guards and others obeying orders. To explore how it was humanly possible for people to behave in this way, Milgram created situations in the laboratory in which the participants increasingly came into conflict with their consciences. These experiments are outlines in Box 4.

Box 4   Experiments on obedience to authority (Milgram, 1974).

Milgram conducted a series of eighteen experiments in which he asked his subjects to act with increasing severity towards another person. The experiments were designed to explore the conditions in which they would or would not comply with the authority of the experimenter.

The subjects, who were recruited by advertisements from a cross section of the population to take part in a scientific study of learning and memory, were instructed to inflict increasing levels of electric shock to a 'learner' who made mistakes in learning a series of paired words. Subjects met the 'learner', who was a confederate of the expe-

rimenter, at the outset. The 'learner' was then strapped into a chair in
the next room and, as the experiment proceeded, his cries of anguish
and his pleas to stop the experiment could be heard. These were in fact
prerecorded and the electric shocks were not actually administered.
The experiments were very realistically staged and each subject had
been given a sample of the kind of electric shock he was about to
administer.

Do you think you would have agreed to participate in such an
experiment? Most people when asked this question reply that they would
not agree to participate, nor do they believe that other people would be
willing to do so. And yet, many people did participate and twenty-six of
forty male subjects in the original experiment administered the highest
shock level on the generator, which was clearly marked 'dangerous'. The
other fourteen refused to continue at an earlier stage.

The procedures in this and subsequent experiments required the
subjects to offend against normal moral codes and, whilst the experiments
created extreme levels of nervous tension, many subjects were, nevertheless, prepared to carry on and accept, or at any rate act on, the definition
of the situation given by the experimenter, to obey him and ignore the
'victim' though he, too, directly appealed to them. (In some of the experiments, the 'victim' was in the room rather than merely heard from the
adjacent room and in these conditions, fewer people were prepared to
administer high levels of shock.)

In all, over one thousand participants come to be involved in these
experiments. Most were male but forty women were also studied. Their
level of obedience was virtually identical to that of the men. Milgram
speculates whether this resulted from the supposed greater willingness of
women to obey being cancelled out by their supposed greater empathy
with people.

In the original design of these experiments group membership was not
of prime concern. However, in some of the experiments the subject
became a member of a peer group. In one variation of the basic design,
two confederates of the experimenter participated with the subject but
were instructed to defy the experimenter's authority and refuse to punish
the 'learner'. This experiment allows us to observe the extent to which
support from fellow group members can release the subject from authoritarian control. The effect of the 'peer rebellion', as Milgram called it,
was very impressive — thirty-six of forty subjects now defied the
experimenter.

Milgram points out that a close analysis of this last mentioned
experiment reveals several factors that contribute to the effectiveness of
the group in influencing the individual subject. He notes:

1 The peers instil in the subject the idea of defying the experimenter. It

1 *Shock generator used in the experiments. Fifteen of the thirty switches have already been depressed.*

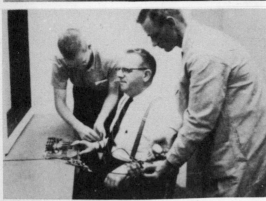

2 *Learner is strapped into chair and electrodes are attached to his wrist. Electrode paste is applied by the experimenter. Learner provides answers by depressing switches that light up numbers on an answer box.*

3 *Subject receives sample shock from the generator.*

4 *Subject breaks off experiment. On right, event recorder wired into generator automatically records switches used by the subject.*

FIGURE 3. *Milgram's experiments on obedience*
SOURCE: *Copyright 1965 Stanley Milgram. From the film obedience, distributed by the New York University Film Division and the Pennsylvania State University, PCR.*

may not have occurred to some subjects as a possibility.

2 The lone subject in previous experiments had no way of knowing whether, if he defies the experimenter, he is performing in a bizarre manner or whether this action is a common occurrence in the laboratory. The two examples of disobedience he sees suggest that defiance is a natural reaction to the situation.

3 The reactions of the defiant confederates define the act of shocking the victim as improper. They provide social confirmation for the subject's suspicion that it is wrong to punish a man against his will [sic], even in the context of a psychological experiment.

4 The defiant confederates remain in the laboratory even after withdrawing from the experiment (they have agreed to answer post-experimental questions). Each additional shock administered by the naive subject then carries with it a measure of social disapproval from the two rebellious confederates.

5 As long as the two confederates participate in the experimental procedure, there is a dispersion of responsibility among the group members for shocking the victim. As the confederates withdraw, responsibility becomes focused on the naive subject.

6 The naive subject is a witness to two instances of disobedience and observes the consequences of defying the experimenter to be minimal.

7 The experimenter's power may be diminished by the very fact of failing to keep the two confederates in line, in accordance with the general rule that every failure of authority to exact compliance to its commands weakens the perceived power of the authority (Homans, 1961).

(Milgram, 1974, pp. 120—121)

Thus, in a situation where subjects have support from others, they can resist external psychological pressures. We have already witnessed this in the Asch paradigm; in the condition where the subject was not the only 'naive' subject he was better able to resist group pressures and to stick to his own perceptions and judgements. In the Milgram experiments, when operating as a member of a peer group, the subject was able to oppose (or liberate himself from) the experimenter's expectations and authority.

One other experiment in this series of obedience studies is particularly relevant in the context of our discussion of the individual and the group. Milgram arranged this experiment in such a way that a confederate actually depressed the lever on the shock generator and the subject was merely engaged in subsidiary tasks. In this condition, thirty-seven of the forty subjects continued to participate in the experiment to the end. As Milgram points out, they felt doubly absolved from responsibility — legitimate authority had given orders but they themselves had not committed any brutality.

What lessons can we learn from these disturbing studies?

In the Nuremberg trials after the Second World War, obedience by a soldier to a command resulting in an unlawful act was defined as a crime and this view has been generally accepted. In other words 'I was only following orders' is no longer consider an excuse for wrongdoing. For instance, those involved in the My Lai massacre in the later Vietnam war were not allowed to claim this defence. And yet, Milgram's subjects carried out an odious task which could certainly be described as unlawful as well as immoral and they engaged in this task without being subjected to propaganda about the iniquities of the 'enemy' that is so characteristic of wartime situations. Ordinary decent people from all walks of life were quickly loosened from their moral moorings, did not act in accordance with their internalized values and engaged in barbarous acts because they perceived the experimenter as an 'authority' figure to whom obedience was due, even though they were appealed to by the 'victim' at the same time. (We shall return to the phenomenon of ignoring a person who needs help when we will discuss 'bystander apathy' in Section III). Whilst the subjects, that is, those who administered the shock, suffered from strain and anxiety and often asked to be allowed to stop, a high proportion nevertheless carried on. One way of explaining such behaviour is by reference to the Freudian concept of *denial* (a largely unconscious process which leads to the rejection of the evidence in front of one's eyes in order to arrive at an explanation which is less damaging to one's self-esteem). For instance, Milgram's subjects could deny to themselves responsibility for their actions since they could see themselves as merely following instructions; they might also blame the 'victim' for the situation (since he is making mistakes in his learning task and therefore has only himself to blame for the consequences).

The experiment I referred to earlier in which the confederate rather than the subject presses the lever on the shock-giving apparatus is perhaps the most disturbing. As Milgram points out, it parallels the kind of situation which had, initially, been the focus of his concern and which prevailed in Nazi Germany where a large bureaucracy cooperated in killing six million people in concentration camps though only relatively few engaged in the actual killing.

Milgram's experiments led to much controversy as to the ethics of carrying out research which puts stress on individuals. However, it is likely that the controversy was fuelled, not simply by the methods of research, but by the unpalatable *results* in that these experiments brilliantly demonstrated that it is the *situations* in which people find themselves rather than their *predispositions* or *character traits* that causes them to act the way they do. In societies like ours where we emphasize an individual's responsibility for his or her own actions such findings are more disturbing than the thought that evil deeds are done by a few pathological people and that the rest of us would never act in this way. Even psychiatrists, when asked what proportion of the subjects they thought would comply with the experimenter's demands, seriously underestimated the levels of obedience actually obtained. Most of them, as indeed did Milgram at the outset, thought that the subjects would cease to administer shock when the victim protested. Almost two-thirds of Milgram's subjects who, you will remember, came from many walks of life, were obedient to the experimenter. This is what Hannah Arendt (1963) categorized as the 'banality of evil' when she criticized the prosecution's effort to depict Eichmann as a sadistic monster rather than as a bureaucrat who sat at a desk and did his job.

It is the peculiar strength of the experimental method that it pin-points the importance of the situational context. The experimenter can create 'conditions' to test whether and to what extent they affect the outcome — in the present case conditions such as whether the 'victim' was in the room or outside, whether the experimenter remained in the room or not, whether there were confederates who defied the experimenter or not, and so on. By contrast, other research methods such as interviews, projective tests or attitude scales focus on individual differences. In a later section (pages 97—100) I shall examine the concept of the *authoritarian personality* one of whose characteristics appears to be undue obedience to authority, not in particular situations, but through a pervasive disposition to respond in this fashion as a result of the child-rearing methods to which they had been exposed.

Conformity and independence

The studies so far reviewed were all concerned, in one way or another, with the influence of the social context (whether created in the laboratory or observed in a women's college) on people's behaviour. In particular, these studies focused on the extent of people's conformity to the expectations of others in their groups. Are we now in a position to understand the nature of conformity and the conditions in which it occurs? What in fact do we mean by conformity? Does it imply unthinking or routine adherence to existing social values or forms of behaviour? Does conformity simply refer to the existence of a consensus about certain issues? We all, at times, conform in these senses but conformity tends to become a 'problem' (and hence a focus of research) only when we think, possibly quite subjectively, that there is too much conformity or, and this is more important, when conformity leads to immoral or illegal actions and/or attitudes which are apparently, contrary to an individual's 'normal' attitudes.

If you think back for a moment to the four major studies we have reviewed, you will remember that Sherif's study dramatically demonstrated the emergence of group norms and their retention by individuals even when no longer in the group. His work is important for providing experimental evidence for this process and, indeed, for establishing that it is possible to study the formation of social norms in the laboratory. Sherif did not use the word 'conformity' for what he observed though the behaviour of his subjects could be described as conformity to group norms (once they were established).

Newcomb's study is rather different from the others in that he observed a large group of people over four years and described the gradual change in attitudes which took place through debates and increased knowledge of social issues. Attitude change was described by him as a function of group membership for, you will recall, he considered it 'normal' to adopt the attitudes of one's group. Again the word 'conformity' was not used, the process being referred to as 'bending towards group expectations'. His work remains important for highlighting the fact that group membership may have different effects according to whether an individual does or does not make a group his or her reference group.

With Asch we moved into a different approach to the problem since he deliberately arranged laboratory situations to put group pressure on individuals to modify their own judgements. He considered such modification of judgements as conformity and furthermore he viewed conformity as a deplorable attribute. He described his conforming subjects as *yielding* to group pressure. Had he thought of conformity as a positive trait, he might have referred to these subjects as *trusting* other people. Those who gave the correct answer he referred to, approvingly, as *independent*. But, as has often been asked, do not the latter conform as well? They may continue to conform to the norms of their society according to which it is not acceptable or usual to defer to the opinions of the majority when these opinions differ from one's own views or judgements. Hence, we can think of the naive subjects in the Asch situation as members of *temporary membership groups* in which some manage to maintain their links with their 'normal' membership and reference groups outside the immediate situation and others do not. These subjects are a 'captive audience' and, as we shall discuss later, may in this respect be said to resemble prisoners of war who are subjected to propaganda and indoctrination. Do all of us then *always* conform but the apparent resisters conform to *other* groups or standards? This is indeed an unanswerable question but Moscovici and Faucheux (1972) hold that 'the only truly independent response in one of Asch's experiments was to leave the room' (p174). When Allen (1975), however, carried out a study in which subjects had the option on each of twelve trials of *abstaining* from making a judgement, he found that subjects did *not* avoid the conflict by abstaining, that is, leaving the psychological field (if not the room), but rather exhibited the same degree of conformity as Asch's subjects. Allen concluded that a dual process is involved in group pressure — to answer rather than stay uncommitted because everyone else answers and, additionally, to agree with (that is, conform to) the group's position. Allen, too, found that, as in the Asch experiments, support for the minority opinion was effective. In other words, when there was social support for abstaining because a confederate of the experimenter abstained, more subjects did, in fact, abstain. But we may both resist and conform at one and the same time in the same situation. Thus we saw in Milgram's studies on obedience to authority that subjects were better able to *resist* his authority when they had the opportunity to *conform* to the norms of resistance projected by his confederates.

Milgram, as we have seen, focused his attention on the effects of authority and distinguished pressure or support from fellow group members from the demands arising from a hierarchical context. In the Asch experiments subjects seem to come under the sway of both these forces — hierarchical authority as represented by the experimenter and pressure from group members towards conformity. Outside the laboratory, in more normal everyday circumstances, we would expect people to argue with and challenge others or to seek clarification of the situation. To leave the room, as Moscovici and Faucheux have suggested, is clearly not the only independent response when faced with a majority one disagrees with.

We will now turn to some other issues which follow on from the research already discussed and which will help us unravel the processes at work when social influence is accepted or rejected.

Public vs private acceptance

In discussing group influence a useful distinction may be made between *public compliance* (with the group norm, the majority opinion or the perceived expectations of the experimenter/leader) and *private agreement* or *private change* (from a prior attitude). Festinger (1953), Kelman (1958) and Jahoda (1959) have stressed the importance of making such a distinction. When individuals are exposed to group pressure, they may publicly conform or not conform to the group. Regardless of this public response, they can privately agree or disagree with the group. Hence the following are possible in response to group expectations.

(a) public conformity and private agreement;
(b) public conformity and private disagreement;
(c) public non-conformity and private disagreement.
(d) public non-conformity and private agreement.

(a) and (c) indicate a correspondence between public and private responses and
(b) and (d) indicate a lack of such correspondence.

Two obstensibly identical responses of public conformity may thus reflect two quite different psychological states and, similarly, public non-conformity also may represent two different private states.

Kelman (1958) has referred to public agreement without private change (that is, in the above terminology, with private disagreement) as *compliance* to group norms for ulterior motives (to gain rewards or to avoid punishment). He further distinguishes *identification* with the group where agreement is public because the person values his or her membership of the group but the private acceptance is temporary and will not be maintained once the person leaves the group. A true private change is referred to by him as *internalization* and implies that an attitude has become part of the person's own value system (because the new information or opinion its in with his or her other attitudes). Once internalized, the attitude will be maintained even when the individual is no longer a member of the group. Festinger (1953) made a similar point. He argues that public conformity will be accompanied by private acceptance only if the person wants to remain a member of the group which is attempting to influence him or her. However, whether a person does or does not wish to remain a member may depend on many factors — whether it is a 'real' group or simply an experimental group with a short life, how attractive the group is to an individual, what other group memberships are open to him or her, and whether he or she is in a position to leave the group? Sometimes people will have to settle for what Kelman referred to as identification — there is public agreement because it is important for a person to remain (for instance to continue in a job or to maintain a marriage) but there is no private agreement.

Is it possible to determine empirically whether a particular group produces only public compliance or both public compliance and private commitment? One way might be to ask a subject to give a public verbal response and at the same time give a private written response hidden from the group. But, since such a response would be seen later by the experimenter, from the subject's point of view it might not be a genuinely private response. Another method would be to compare the public response given under group pressure and the response when the group is not present. However if both responses denote agreement with the group position one might still not be able to conclude that private acceptance occurred at the time when the public response was made. As we shall shortly discuss when considering the influence a minority may achieve, private change may have occurred later through different psychological processes operating initially at a latent level. There is, of course, also the possibility of interviewing subjects after experimental sessions, but here, too, memory may be incomplete or censored by the individual's conscious or unconscious attempts at maintaining his or her self-image. If you think back to Sherif's experiments on the autokinetic effect (described in Box 1) you may conclude that he obtained lasting rather than merely temporary change in that his subjects carried the norms and ranges they developed initially into later experimental situations. Of course, as you also remember, the situation was totally ambiguous and subjects initially had no previous norms on which to rely or to which to return, once they were away from the group, and this is rather different from most other situations in which people find themselves.

Festinger (1957) in his 'cognitive dissonance theory' suggests that an inconsistency or imbalance *either* between the values, beliefs or attitudes we hold *or* between such 'cognitions' and our behaviour leads to unpleasant tensions which we seek to reduce. When the dissonance is caused by incompatible cognitions we can change some of them to bring them into line with others. Where tension, however, results from a clash between our views and how we behave then, he suggests, it is our views which will have to adjust since behaviour, once engaged in, cannot be wished away. He, therefore, holds that attitude change may *follow* voluntary counter-attitudinal public behaviour. In other words, one way of reducing dissonance, is to change one's view or attitudes and, therefore, the very act of public commitment may also produce private acceptance.

However, you will remember, in the Asch experiment (Box 3) the overt agreement with the group led to private acceptance in only a few subjects. His interviews showed that it was unusual for subjects to change their *perception* of the stimulus (which we might equate with private acceptance), they merely agreed with the group even though they thought the group was wrong. (And, of course, even those who reported a perceptual change may have 'rationalized' their agreement with the group which is another way of reducing cognitive dissonance.) There is confirmation of the temporary nature of the effect of Asch's procedure from Luchins and Luchins (1955) who found that when, after the group session, the entire set of lines was re-administered to the subject in the absence of the confederates, no mistakes occurred. This is, perhaps, not very surprising since it is difficult to imagine a private commitment to an issue such as which lines are equal to a standard line when the facts (in the absence of group pressure) are unequivocal.

Nevertheless, this point may not be entirely straighforward. Again it is Festinger who makes an interesting comment. According to his theory of cognitive dissonance, the attractiveness of the chosen alternative (in this case, to agree with the group) increases after the decision and the attractiveness of the unchosen possibility (in this case, to disagree with the group) decreases. This implies that a subject who has adopted a certain position may maintain this response during the experiment *and* in later experimental sessions. Though perhaps, if such a response pattern occurs, it need not be explained in terms of commitment — another emotive word; rather we may think of it as the formation of a response *norm* in the way that Sherif demonstrated. Such a response norm can also be viewed as face-saving and as reducing post-decision dissonance.

However, commitment to our involvement with an issue *prior* to any attempt at influencing the person, whether through group pressure or persuasive communications, may affect the outcome. Thus, Jahoda (1959) points out that 'one and the same position taken by different individuals can have completely different meanings, that is, different antecedents, different contexts, and different consequences'. She adds: 'position-taking on an issue in which the individual has intellectual and emotional investment is psychologically so different a process from position-taking on an issue which is not so invested, that they must be assumed to manifest different regularities'. In her analysis of the empirical work on conformity Jahoda alerts us to the danger of taking too simplistic a view of the process and its outcomes. Figure 4 shows the eight acts which can result from the influence process when a person's initial position is taken into account.

Public vs private response

So far I have discussed the relationship between public response and private acceptance without focusing specifically on whether a person's behaviour was observed in a public or a private condition though, where

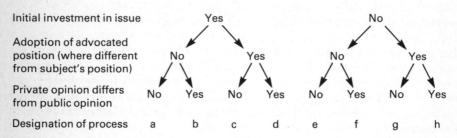

Explanatory comments: a, b, c, d refer to persons with an initial intellectual or emotional involvement with an issue.

a   denotes a person who does not change his or her mind and is at ease with him or herself about the final position taken.

b   implies a person who adheres to his or her original position but feels less comfortable with it than previously.

c   describes a person who changes his or her mind as a result of a campaign or group pressure and who is at ease about this change.

d   describes a person who complies under some pressure but maintains his or her private opinion.

e, f, g, h refer to persons who had no intellectual or emotional involvement with an issue.

e   denotes a person not affected by a campaign or group pressure.

f   denotes a person who has changed his or her opinion privately only – on the face of it an unlikely position.

g   denotes a common response where there is no initial involvement in an issue.

h   denotes a person who maintains his or her private opinion even though there is no initial investment in the issue, a less common response.

FIGURE 4.   Types of conformity and independence (adopted from Jahoda, 1959)

subjects had the opportunity to respond in public *and* in private, the private response was taken by psychologists as being indicative of the person's private acceptance. However, the question has been raised as to whether the *mode of response* itself will affect the issue. A *public response* would be a response given aloud in a face-to-face group as in the original Asch experiment. The term *private response* generally refers to a response given anonymously and in private, for instance in a postal questionnaire rather than in a face-to-face situation. There is a famous example in the social psychological literature on prejudice in which there was a marked disparity between the publicly and privately given responses of hotel owners to the issue of whether or not they would accommodate Chinese people. La Piere (1934) found the hotel owners stated in response to a questionnaire that they would not accommodate Chinese people, but when they came face-to-face with a Chinese couple travelling with an American very few refused to do so. Several explanations can be found to account for these differences. An individual may have a range of attitudes on a given issue and different situations may elicit the display of only some of them. On the other hand, the *mode of response* (filling in an anonymous questionnaire as compared to having to make a decision on what to do in a face-to-face situation) may also affect the response. Some studies have been undertaken by social psychologists where the mode of response has been made the independent variable. Thus, for instance, Levy (1960) compared conformity in a face-to-face situation with one where the alleged responses of other group members were shown on a screen but the subject was on his own and gave his response in private. Levy found more conformity in face-to-face groups than in the simulated groups and so did other researchers. However, it is not obvious what one is to make of such results. Two possible interpretations can be put forward: either that people conform more on public occasions to avoid disagreements irrespective of their private views, or that a face-to-face group may simply be more convincing than simulated responses. Hence the fact that the response is given in relative privacy may be irrelevant and may not account for the observed variations in conformity in the two conditions.

Personal predisposition vs situational determinants

The original Asch studies, whilst emphasizing the situational factors which affect conformity, have also shown that individuals vary in the extent to which they conform to the group. Similarly, research on responses to persuasive communications has also demonstrated some individual differences in susceptibility to influence.

However, a good deal of research on demographic and personality factors, designed to pinpoint the psychological characteristics of individuals who may be predisposed to yield to or to resist influence from group members or from persuasive communications, has not led to any clear-cut results. For instance, it has been asked whether age or sex have something to do with a person's persuasibility. Age, except in the first few years of life when children tend to accept influence more readily than later, does not appear to be a very significant variable. As regards sex, in so far as any differences are found, some studies showed that women were somewhat more easily influenced than men (Hovland and Janis, 1959). However, such findings may be of historical interest only and no longer true, given that the self-esteem and self-reliance of women is greater than it was twenty-five years ago. Sistrunk and McDavid (1971) have also shown that the results in earlier studies were an artifact of the items chosen: when the subject matter was familiar to women, they did not conform to the incorrect majority views and, indeed, the same is true of men. Appropriate knowledge, as we have also seen in discussing Perrin and Spencer's (1981) replication of the Asch studies, reduces the susceptibility of both sexes to false majority opinion. Investigations of the role of intelligence have given contradictory results, not perhaps surprisingly, since an intelligent person may be more capable of paying attention to and comprehending persuasive information but may also have the knowledge or alertness to resist yielding to it. Characteristics such as a person's degree of self-esteem or anxiety (often manipulated and temporarily changed by the experimenter) also produce a confusing picture when related to his or her susceptibility to influence. Again, the internal mediating processes may work against each other: anxiety may make people more prone to yield to persuasion or group pressure but less susceptible because they fail to pay attention or because anxiety may hinder comprehension.

The focus on personality factors has been virtually abandoned because of a growing awareness that yielding or remaining independent do not represent unitary character traits which an individual either possesses or lacks. More fruitful insights have been gained by focusing on the situational aspects which may determine the *extent* of the group's influence. Thus, psychologists have studied the size and unanimity of the group; the cohesiveness and attractiveness of the group; the individual's status (do leaders conform more or less to group norms? — (page 65); the extremity of the norms presented (the more extreme the norms, the greater the conflict in the deviant subject); the nature of the task (visual stimuli as in Asch or opinion or information items) and, as has already been mentioned, the subject's competence (the more competent at a task the subject is, the less conformity to erroneous judgements occurs.) Similarly, as we shall see in Section II a number of factors (beyond predisposition) affect the extent to which conformity to persuasive communications is achieved. Thus the structure of a communication, the credibility of the communicator, the type of issue, and the channel through which the communication is presented are all likely to affect the outcome. In particular, we shall see that it is important to take into account both an individual's primary groups and the wider social system when looking at the way in which individuals react to influence attempts. For instance, Hovland *et al.* (1953) stressed the *salience* of group norms to the issue presented. (Group norms are salient to people if they are the norms of their *reference groups*, to use the terminology employed earlier in this section).

Much of the research following on from Asch has focused on conformity, its nature and the conditions in which it is most likely to occur. But, quite early on, in fact in Asch's first series of experiments, *non-conformity* was explored. Thus, as we have seen, when one other member of the group gave the correct response, the naive subject's ability to resist the erroneous majority was considerably increased (Asch, 1952).

Can we define non-conformity? In an ideal world I would be able to give you agreed definitions of such terms as independence, non conformity, anti-conformity or dissent. However, these terms, like the concept of conformity, have been as variously employed by psychologists as by people in general. Disagreement with the group may indicate a spirit of independence, or conformity to a partner in the group, or conformity to reference groups beyond one's immediate membership group.

Allen (1975), amongst others, has carried out a series of experiments on the factors affecting independence from group judgements. His particular focus was the effect of social support for the subject's *private* beliefs and perceptions. The stimuli he used ranged from visual items to opinion and knowledge statements. He concluded that the response subjects give is largely determined by the *meaning* they ascribe to the situation. In his view, conformity is reduced because the social support a subject receives from a partner instigates a process of cognitive restructuring that results in a different interpretation of the stimulus. Thus one important function of the social supporter (or partner as Allen calls him) may be to provide an independent confirmation of physical and social reality when the subject is confronted with anomalous behaviour from the group. In this way, the subject's dependence on the majority for information and or normative expectations (a distinction made by Deutsch and Gerard 1955) or for rewards is reduced, as is his conformity to the majority. The subject's relationship with his partner also influences the outcome. Both Asch (1955) and Allen and Wilder (reported in Allen, 1975) set up experiments in which the partner 'deserted' the subject and began to agree with the group halfway through the experimental session. In both sets of experiments this led to increased conformity to the group by the subject after the 'desertion'. Allen explains these results by arguing that, initially, the credibility of the partner had increased as a consequence of his agreement with the subject. When however, he begins to agree with the group, the group is re-evaluated and *its* credibility is increased.

Both a person's disposition and situational variables would appear to determine the *degree* of an individual's dissent from or agreement with a group. Thus, it is virtually impossible to classify behaviour as conformist or independent *unless* one understands the meaning the situation has for the individual (as Jahoda (1959) had already pointed out) and the implications it has for his or her self-image. Allen concludes that people's ultimate response is the outcome of the balancing of situational factors (the support they have, the ambiguity and nature of the stimulus, etc.) and their initial perception or opinion. One might add that the meaning an experimental or real life situation has also depends on people's goals: are they trying to achieve the completion of a task, the solving of a problem and/or do they wish to be popular or successful? The meaning of the situation may also depend on the cultural expectations people have. Noelle-Neumann (1984) suggests that there may be cultural distinctions in the extent to which people seek agreement between their publicly voiced opinions and their private views. She suggests that in Germany (as compared to the U.S.A.) 'there is a strong tendency for the individual to make the inside and the outside, publicly expressed opinion and private opinion, agree with each other' (p. X).

Majority and minority influence

In the preceding sections we have seen in the research by Asch (1952) and Allen (1975) that a minority of two (as compared to a lone individual) is better placed to *resist* the influence of the majority in a group and remain independent. However, in 1969 the preoccupation of experimental psychologists with conformity gave way to a new question: how can an individual or a minority not just resist the majority but *influence* it? This question has generated considerable research and theorizing in the last fifteen years; research is still continuing and many issues remain unexplained or have given rise to alternative theoretical models. We will also need to explore the extent to which the laboratory research reflects how minorities operate in the real world.

For quite some time prior to the first experiments on minority influence (reported in Box 5) Moscovici in France had been interested in innovation and creativity and how, over a period of time, the novel ideas of original thinkers came to influence the thinking, vocabulary, cultural beliefs or images of the world of successive generations. He referred to a coherent set of *shared* cultural beliefs (whether newly emerging or of long-standing) as *social representations* of the world and such shared social representations are seen as providing a shared 'reality' and order for people which enables them to communicate with each other and make sense of their lives in terms of such social representations.

Moscovici (1961/76) developed these ideas in following the spread of psychoanalytic concepts and ways of thinking from their use by psychologists and other professionals to their appearance in popular books, newspapers, television or films and in the language and thought processes of 'ordinary' people who came to perceive and explain to themselves everyday phenomena in terms of psychoanalytic concepts such as the notion of repression or of unconscious motivation. They had made such terms, consciously or unconsciously, part of their world view. Whilst Moscovici then had a long-standing interest in the diffusion of the revolutionary ideas and theories of outstanding thinkers like Freud *over time*, when he turned to experimentation he focused, of necessity, at any rate initially, on the *short-term* influence of a minority in a small laboratory group engaged in banal tasks. But the innovating minority in the laboratory group resembled the innovating thinkers Moscovici studied in not having any power base from which to influence others in the group.

It is interesting to speculate why his initial experiment aroused so much interest among social psychologists and led to a new research tradition. Whilst he and his colleagues used an experimental situation which could be replicated by others, this alone might not explain the widespread interest which these experiments aroused, particularly in Europe. Perhaps the changing social climate which we already identified as affecting the responses of subjects in the Asch paradigm, also affected the research interests of social psychologists.

In their first experiment on the influence of a minority on the majority members of a group, Moscovici, Lage and Naffrechoux (1969) demonstrated that a *consistent* minority is able to exert a remarkable degree of influence even when it lacks such characteristics as power, status, or idiosyncrasy credit (Hollander, 1958 — see page 65).

Box 5   Experiments on minority influence (Moscovici, Lage and Naffrechoux, 1969).

Moscovici *et al.* conducted an experiment in which subjects were asked to indicate the colour of a slide they were shown and, as a diversion, to estimate its brightness on a five-point scale. Six subjects estimated the colour and brightness in sequence and they were asked to make thirty-six judgements. All slides were blue but the brightness was varied by adding filters. The subjects had been tested to make sure they had normal eyesight. Of the six subjects, two were paid confederates who were instructed to call the slides green on all trials. Thus, they were a minority who saw green where everyone else saw blue and they were *consistent* throughout. The results were that the naive subjects in this condition called the stimulus slides green in 8.42% of the trials and thirty-two percent of all subjects reported to have seen a 'green' slide at least once. In the control condition without confederates the slides were referred to as green in only 0.25% of the judgements made.

In a second condition, the confederates were *inconsistent*. They called the stimulus slides green twenty-four times and blue twelve times in random order. The effect on the naive subjects in this condition was not statistically significant (1.25% of the judgements).

Numerous studies since then have supported the main finding of these experiments that consistent minorities will exert influence whilst inconsistent behaviour will not bring about a significant change in the majority's perceptions or points of view. However, it also became apparent that consistency is not the only factor involved when minorities influence the opinions of the majority and I will discuss some of the factors which have been identified as affecting the outcome.

How can we account for the effects produced by a consistent minority? Initially, the influence of the minority was explained as resulting from the minority first creating a conflict with the majority by challenging its norms and then providing a consistent alternative norm for them to consider (Moscovici *et al.*, 1969; Moscovici and Faucheux, 1972; Moscovici, 1976). The minority, therefore, has to be *active*, rather than resemble the dependent, helpless, disorientated naive subject at whom the majority targets its influence in the typical conformity experiment. A consistent style was seen as crucial to the influence of an active minority since a consistent minority is *perceived* as confident, competent, coherent and distinctive. However, subsequent studies came to the conclusion that consistency is a necessary but not always a sufficient condition for minority influence to occur. For instances, a very rigid style which makes the minority appear dogmatic rather than a flexible style of argument or a large discrepancy between the position advocated by the minority and that of the target majority may cut across the effects of consistency and affect the outcome.

Thus, Mugny (1975) found that a flexible style of negotiation proved more effective when differences in opinion were large, whereas a rigid style of negotiation proved more effective when the majority held a position close to that advocated by the minority. The degree to which a minority is effective may also be influenced by the wider context beyond the immediate group — that is, whether it advocates a position which is in accord with the spirit of the time (see, for instance, Paicheler, 1979; and Maass *et al.*, 1982). In real life contexts, minority groups, too, are more effective when they press views which fit changing social conditions or fit in with views which begin to emerge more generally. Thus the anti-war movement in the United States in the 1960s was successful in exerting influence and the current ecological movement is gaining adherents in many countries. Maass *et al.* (1982) use the term *single* and *double* minorities, a terminology subsequently also used by other researchers. Single minorities are those who deviate from the majority in terms of their beliefs, double minorities, in addition may be categorized as belonging to an *outgroup*. Experimental evidence suggests that double minorities are less effective since an outgroup is less likely to be perceived as a valid reference group and both single and double minorities are less influential if what they advocate runs counter to the spirit of the time, for instance, when they advocate a return to the death penalty in a country where the majority does not favour this view.

Has the research on the diversity of factors which constitute minority influence stimulated theoretical discussion? We have already seen that the effects of a consistent and distinctive minority are thought to depend on the majority *attributing* certain qualities to the minority.

Moscovici (1980) further suggests that the influence of the minority may be at a latent (indirect) rather than at a manifest (direct) level. He describes the former as conversion, the latter as compliance (without inner conviction). He emphasizes that both minorities and majorities exert influence, that the views of the former are not automatically rejected because they are contrary to the majority's norms, nor are the views of the latter accepted without resistance because they agree with the norm. If no change can be observed in response to a minority position on a direct, outward level, some alteration may nevertheless have taken place on an indirect, latent level and may become manifest later. Thus when in the previously described experiment (Moscovici *et al.*, 1969) the same slides are shown again *without* any influence attempts by the minority (subjects individually wrote down their judgements) *more* slides were seen as green, that is, remarkably, the answers were not simply a verbal agreement with a consistent minority but demonstrated a continued influence corresponding to a change in perceptual organization. In other words, the minority's views or actions may raise doubts and dissonance which continue to work in the mind of the individual. In that way, Moscovici hypothesizes, the latent 'conversion' processes initiated by the minority may have a greater effect on a 'deeper' level than the overt, and possibly temporary, 'compliance' effects resulting from the influence of the majority. It should be noted that many experimenters have used the terms public and private change as interchangeable with manifest and latent change. Strictly speaking, any discrepancy between public and private responses should refer to the extent an individual is prepared for others to be aware of his position. Manifest and latent change, on the other hand, refers to the extent an individual accepts an advocated position and the presumed permanency of the effect, latent refering to the more deep-seated and therefore more important and long-term effect (internalization).

Public and private responses arise from *interpersonal* aspects (for instance perceived social pressure); the terms manifest and latent refer to *intrapersonal* aspects (the extent to which the individual has altered his cognitions).

The research on minority influence has hence led to a shift from explanations in terms of *interpersonal* influence processes to *intrapersonal* cognitive processes operating over a period of time. This shift also implies a greater awareness of the complexity of the processes involved and a change of focus from social control and conformity to social change and innovation. In this way, the research on minority influence in groups has proved to be a corrective to the earlier concern with conformity.

Majorities and minorities (at any rate in the laboratory) seem to work through different processes. The information coming from a minority source is likely to be processed more *actively* (because it causes cognitive and social conflict and generates more counter arguments); the information coming from the majority is processed more passively (since the fact of there being a majority is hypothesized as making the minority dependent on the majority and they will 'unthinkingly' accept its influence). This has been referred to as the 'dual process model' that is, it rests on the assumption that minorities and majorities produce qualitatively different effects through different underlying processes. There is support for this view from experimental studies (for a review, see Moscovici, 1980).

But why should the minority and the majority achieve influence in such different ways? It is likely that being faced with a majority with whom one disagrees is more stressful than being faced with a minority because in the first case (for instance in the Asch situation) an individual faces both a challenge to his or her own position *and* the likelihood of disapproval from the majority. By contrast, the minority does not have this kind of immediate impact and is less threatening and thus the majority may be more willing and able to consider the minority's point of view. Nemeth and Wachtler (1983) suggest that *majority* influence will lead to the minority either following the majority exactly or remaining independent. They hypothesize that where the influencing agent is a member of a *minority*, subjects would not react in this way but would reassess their positions, would be under less stress and might be likely to *adopt a novel position*, that is, one which is different both from their own original position and the one advocated. In their experiment subjects were asked to resolve an embedded figures task (that is, find figures which are hidden in the overall design). In both the conformity and the minority paradigm the confederates always found the same two embedded figures. The subjects in the former complied with the majority, in the latter condition the subjects were less likely to name these two embedded figures but found a great number of additional figures which had not been proposed by the confederates. In other words, the challenge posed by the minority led others in the group to think for themselves and the authors suggest that this experiment shows that the influence of the minority can lead to creativity and innovation.

However, the 'dual process model' has not remained unchallenged. Latané with various co-workers (Latané and Nida, 1980; Latané and

Wolf, 1981) has proposed a *theory of social impact* which may account for the reciprocal influence of majorities and minorities in laboratory settings. Previous work, as we have seen, has suggested that the influence of the minority and the majority require different explanations. Thus the impact of the majority can be viewed as resulting from its greater ability to establish social reality and from the dependency of the minority on the majority. The influence of the minority has been attributed to its consistent behavioural style (perhaps its only weapon), denoting confidence and commitment and thus becoming the focus of attention.

Social impact theory, by contrast, hypothesizes that one common influence process is responsible for both conformity and minority influence. Rather than taking the group as a whole, it views the majority and the minority as separate sources of influence in the same social field. Each of these sub-groups (or a single individual) is seen as a potential source of influence for the other. Whatever position an individual assumes with respect to a given issue, he or she will be an active participant in the influence process and the influence of majorities and minorities is seen as simultaneous and reciprocal. Thus, where majorities and minorities are of comparable size (that is, where two factions with opposing views have been created in a group) one would expect that any emerging consensus would be less one-sided than it would be if there were no minority position advocated. Unlike Moscovici's model, however, social impact theory does not suggest that the minority's influence will be more than proportional to its strength, nor does this theory address itself to the question of whether and how an individual or a minority can maintain their original position. Going beyond the laboratory, Latané and Wolf (1981) note that the influence of the minority is based on the fact that in changing times and conditions the views of the minority may be more realistic than those of the outmoded majority. They thus may serve as the trigger to the 'conversion' effects identified by Moscovici (1980). As they put it: 'Like the child who first remarked on the Emperor's lack of clothes, non-elite minorities may be effective mainly when majorities have blinded themselves to naked reality. If the Emperor were in fact dressed the child would, of course, be ignored' (Latané and Wolf, 1981, p. 452).

If you think back over this section you may conclude that minorities are potentially very effective change agents, producing private change rather than overt compliance and that such change is brought about by intense cognitive activity. This would be a fair conclusion and yet we can see all around us the continuing effects of pressures towards conformity. Two points can be made:

Firstly, these experiments were designed to explore minority influences and the cognitive and other processes through which minorities created their effects. They were effective, as we have seen, because the experimenter *instructed* the minority to be active and present a view which differed consistently from that held by the majority. Such explorations do not nullify the earlier experiments which showed how conformity comes about and how the minority can be helpless and overwhelmed by the majority when the majority adopts a consistent style and position. The more recent studies focusing on minority effects merely demonstrate that minority influences can also be brought into play and made to be effective.

Secondly, as some authors have pointed out (for instance, Mugny, 1982) by agreeing with the minority a person runs the risk of being identified with it and thereby assuming a minority (or outgroup) status. If the problem put to a group is a realistic one, this is an important consideration and may make people hesitate to adopt a minority opinion. The kind of realistic issues Mugny, a Swiss psychologist, used were attitudes to 'guest workers' and to compulsory military service. We might, therefore, as with conformity experiments, expect some differences according to whether in an experiment the *mode of response* was public or private; nevertheless, if people hesitate to join a minority publicly, they may still be affected by the *conversion* processes hypothesized by Moscovici. In the world at large, of course, there is another factor: arguments on important issues, such as in Switzerland the position of 'guest workers' or compulsory military service, do not occur just in a one-off laboratory experiment. The issues are widely debated in the media, in pubs, in the family, among friends and, in Switzerland, voted on in public referenda. The ultimate outcome, therefore, cannot be pinpointed in a laboratory experiment using a group convened for a one-off session. Maass and Clark (1984) have pointed to the absence of field studies, that is, of systematic observations of how minorities conduct themselves in the world at large in the research on minority influence; furthermore, the complexity of the phenomenon and the lack of theoretical integration make it difficult to be precise about the relevance these studies have for real life. But much of what these researchers have explored is thought-provoking and provides lessons for the innovator, change-agent, or the members of a pressure group. For instance, we have seen that *active* minorities can stimulate the majority to rethink its position; that 'latent' minority effects may be more powerful in the longer term than 'manifest' conformity effects; that the style of advocacy (rigid or flexible) may be variously appropriate; that the wider social context affects the extent to which the minority can hope to be successful, be it that the particular social context favours originality or because, as Latané and Wolf (1981) put it, changing times make the views of the minority more realistic. The lessons for a minority intent on achieving influence are to choose an appropriate style, knowing when to intervene and when to press its views. Minorities, as we all know, do have effects — new ideas, innovations, reforms or revolutions would not be possible without deviants or minorities who propose alternative goals or means.

But given that there are such lessons we still need to ask how far the research on minority influence has tapped what goes on in the world around us.

First of all, one should perhaps remember that not all minorities set out to exert influence. Not all religions, for instance, seek converts (though they may wish to strengthen belief within their own group).

Secondly, the research described in this section focuses on minorities who lack *status*. The minority in a typical experiment is simply designated as such by the experimenter and asked to argue for a view which (it has been established or it is assumed) the majority in the group do not share. We have seen that this lack of status may be emphasized by creating double minorities — that is, the minority view is projected by members of an out-group with whom the majority members do not identify and whom they do not accept as a valid point of reference. But, by contrast, in the social world outside the laboratory, there are *élites* who, though numerically in a minority, do not lack status or power and who may exert considerable influence. In fact, the example of élites highlights a confusion or, at any rate, an inconsistency in the use of the word minority. A minority can be, firstly, the numerically smaller section in a group and the dividing factor may be sex, religion, race, class and so on. Secondly, a group may be designated as a minority because its members hold views which are not shared by the majority; and, thirdly the word minority is nowadays often used to describe those whose position in society is weak — be they women (though numerically in a majority) or blacks (also in the majority in South Africa and in several states in the United States) or members of other persecuted or economically weak groups, whether numerically in the minority or not.

Thirdly, we need to ask how minorities who do want to exert influence operate in the world. How do feminists, gay liberationists, 'pro-lifers,' animal rights campaigners and so on attempt to achieve their aims? How do small politically motivated groups proceed to 'capture' trade unions or political parties in order to obtain disproportionate influence? Can we really understand the effects of pressure groups by reference to their cognitive styles? Certainly such groups would need to know precisely what they want to advocate and to achieve and to put their views across effectively. But they would also need commitment to their cause and singlemindedness (factors pointed to in the research on minorities) and they would need to be *organized*, for instance, they might meet as a caucus before a meeting of a whole group to decide on the tactics to be used. In other words, successful minorities do not simply engage in persuasion, they create a powerbase for themselves.

Fourthly, we need to ask whether the main question to be explored concerns the actions of the minority group. Initially, a militant minority may well have an advantage and gain the upper hand. It takes time for the majority to grasp what is happening and for groups opposed to the minority to crystallize and speak on behalf of the 'silent majority'. But gradually, people may begin to realize that they are being challenged, subverted, threatened by the minority *and* realize that there are others like them who are experiencing a similar sense of dislocation. The attitude of 'live and let live' which is basic to social consensus collapses and the majority will confront the minority. Such a backlash can currently be observed in the re-assertion of its views by the 'moral majority' in the United States.

The research on minority influence which at present is mainly based on laboratory experiments does not capture such a scenario in which the majority eventually actively reacts to the challenge posed by the minority. Of course, as has been pointed out, where the views pressed by the minority are in the spirit of the time such a reaction may not occur and what was a minority view establishes itself, possibly in a modified version, as the majority consensus. But, whether or not influence attempts by the minority are in the spirit of the time, we are not equally receptive to all attempts at persuasion. For instance, we may consider a particular religious group to be part of the 'lunatic fringe' and feel immune to its efforts in gaining followers. There are many minority groups who have very little influence and precisely because of that also do not call forth a reaction from the majority.

Conclusions to Section 1

We have seen that the word 'group' refers to many entities — to large or small, formal or informal groups; to groups in which a person is present or groups taken as a reference point whether or not an individual is physically present in them; to ephemeral experimental groups or groups which have a long history; and to groups which a person joins voluntarily or is thrust into by race or nationality. Whilst the word 'group' is used in all these contexts it might be more correct to refer at all times to 'people in groups' or 'people relating to each other in groups' or some such form of words. The word 'group' reifies (literally: makes a thing of) something which does not exist except in terms of the effects those participating (by their physical or mental presence) have on each other, the meanings they attribute to such interactions and the intrapsychic cognitive restructuring which may result. But, as Jahoda (1982) points out though 'we are all unique individuals . . . no experience, thought, feeling or achievement is conceivable as the creation of a single mind'. Thus, even though we may have ceased to look on groups as *things* — out there to be observed or participated in — they are still a meaningful focus in social psychology, and, having made the point concerning the danger of reification, I shall continue to use the word as a shorthand reference to the relationships of people in groups.

The word 'member', too, can have different meanings for the individual concerned. How fully people consider themselves to be members of a group (and hence the extent to which they are likely to be influenced by others in the group) may depend on the group's structure, the context in which it exists or evolves, the extent to which membership in other groups is available to people, their dispositions and knowledge.

The effects that group membership is likely to have (on perceptions, attitudes, values, judgements or behaviour, and so on) depend on the characteristics of the group as they mesh with the needs or characteristics of its members. The intra-group effects may also be affected by the wider social context in which they occur. The precise outcomes of such interactions are, therefore, difficult to predict. The observed outcomes, as we have seen, are also, in part, an artefact of the particular questions one asks — such as whether one is concerned with the conditions in which conformity occurs or with the exploration of independence or deviance. Furthermore, within such broader categories, the precise manipulation of the independent variable and what is accepted as the dependent variable, for instance, a response in private or public, also affect the outcome.

Because of the complexity arising from the interplay of all these factors (and at what point we focus on them) it is not possible to decide which of the influence processes we have discussed is most fundamental. Thus, social comparison processes, conformity pressures, the stimulus emanating from strong minority opinions or the view that 'social impact' owes something to all participants, all describe processes for which there is experimental evidence and which may go on *simultaneously*. The focus on any one of them results from the (necessarily) partial view a researcher or theorist takes. The first and last of these processes are, of course, more inclusive and probably can be applied to the understanding of most ingroup behaviour and experience. The others arise more specifically from the issues to which their proponents have addressed themselves.

We have seen that the questions social psychologists have asked about the effects of group membership have changed over a period of time. Questions concerning the formation and maintenance of individual and group norms (Sherif, 1936) were followed by the exploration of the effects of membership as compared to reference groups (Newcomb, 1952). The psychological experience of group pressure (Asch, 1952) proved a focus for much subsequent research both on conformity to and on independence from group norms and a shift in emphasis from interpersonal influence processes to intrapersonal cognitive restructuring.

Underlying all these questions and the different influence processes which have been identified, there are basically two aspects which underpin the explanations given for the effects which group members have on each other (and they are not mutually exclusive).

The first kind of explanation derives from the observable fact that we are born with predispositions and attributes which mark us out as social beings and that our early dependence on other people for survival strengthens and develops such dispositions. In this sense it is 'natural' that we seek out others, congregate with others (even when, as I pointed out in the Introduction, there is no practical necessity to do so) and, the corollary to such assumptions, adjust to other people as well as expect other people to adjust to our views, preferences or behaviours. Social life would not be possible unless this were so and this is what is encapsulated in the study of 'groups'. As I have pointed out the importance of the concept of group rests on the fact that primary groups arise spontaneously (and can very easily be established even in artificial laboratory situations). Where they exceed more than about twelve members, they tend to split into new groups as they become too large for all members to have face-to-face contacts. It is no accident that groups in which cohesion is important rarely exceed a dozen members — Christ's disciples (and here one member became a deviant), the cricket eleven or a football team all testify to this fact.

The second kind of explanation focuses on the power relationships within groups. Thus, the majority in a group may be perceived as powerful 'norm senders' since they have sanctions at their disposal (disapproval or rejection). These sanctions are effective in producing the outcomes desired by the majority precisely because deviant or potentially deviant group members may be psychologically dependent on the majority for information and/or approval. In this sense, an explanation in terms of power is entirely compatible with stating that 'we bend towards group expectations' (Newcomb, 1952) because it is human nature to be social and to adopt the attitudes of the group or groups of which one is a member. But, as we have seen, when one focuses on the influence of the minority, then one cannot speak of power but one needs to have recourse to describing its effect in terms of a chain of cognitive restructuring processes. The concept of power tends to refer to position, status, privileged access to information or the weight of numbers, that is, the resources which make sanctions possible. In that sense, minorities do not have power and, insofar as they are effective, achieve influence through stimulating rethinking in the majority. However, as I pointed out, in the social world at large this is not necessarily how a minority gains influence. What a successful minority actually may do, for instance the members of a C.P. 'cell', is to attempt to gain access to key positions in a union so that the minority has a power base and access to knowledge and power.

Power is primarily a sociological concept, referring to aspects inherent in the social structure (such as class divisions or other inequalities in access to resources). In Section II I will return to this point when we discuss leadership, a word which denotes success in the psychological process of deliberately influencing others, a process which is frequently associated with and, indeed, at times is dependent on, the power arising from a formal position in a social hierarchy. Experimenters, of course, are also often in a position where they are seen as leaders: they set the scene by devising the experiment; they represent 'science' and they are 'in the know', unlike their *subjects* — a really revealing word in this context — and they may have a formal position in the hierarchy of status and power as lecturers or heads of department or have 'real' sanctions at their disposal, such as a requirement for students to put in a certain number of hours as experimental subjects to gain a 'credit' for their course.

When we refer to power in the sense of having a privileged or influential position in the social structure, it might be better to refer to the exercise of power as *social control* rather than as *social influence*. The latter arises in the interaction between people and is a much more inclusive term and independent of whether or not there are asymmetric power positions in the group. It is the word used throughout this first part of the book (and in the literature on which it is based). However, these two terms are not as far apart as one might imagine. Social control is not only based on power but on using 'normal' social influence processes to attempt to change the attitudes or behaviour of people in a predetermined direction. This will be the topic of Section II of this book. Before turning to Section II, however, we need to take stock of the progress we have made.

First of all, can we now define the concept of group? I do not think that we can give *one* definition. We have seen that there are many different kinds of groups and that research has largely focused on the influence processes at work, whether these are intraindividual or interindividual. These in turn are affected by the wider context in which the group exists (the societal level) and structural aspects of the group itself, whether these derive from the societal level or are imposed by the experimenter, who might, for instance, arrange an experiment so that minorities and majorities with asymmetrical power relationships are created in the laboratory situation.

Many recent textbooks do not give a definition of groups but are prepared to define aspects of groups or group membership such as group norms, group structure or group cohesiveness. Where a definition is advanced it is often immediately challengeable. For instance, Barton *et al.* (1974) define a group as: 'Two or more individuals who are interdependent on one or more dimensions and who perceive the existence of the group and their membership in it.' Whilst we would need to define 'interdependent' to make sense of the first part of this statement we know that the second part is wrong: influence processes *can* be at work without the individual being aware of this — a matter demonstrated as early as the 1930s by Sherif's studies on the formation of norms. It is, of course, true that people are mostly conscious of being members of groups — of reference groups such as the British or *Guardian* readers or of membership groups (which, possibly also serve as reference groups) such as a team, or a family or a self-help group.

The evidence for their membership derives from their sharing, or coming to share, *common norms* about issues of importance to them, whether or not they are aware of this process. This is why I opened our study of groups with Sherif's study of the development of norms. If no such consensus arises over a period of time, the group will not maintain itself as a *meaningful psychological focus* in its members' life. A group may in such circumstances maintain a formal existence (such as an empty but non-dissolved marriage) or it may disintegrate (though mainly in the short-term, as we have seen, people may conform overtly to group norms (compliance) and maintain their private views). We have also seen that where there is a felt need for change and an active minority to stimulate rethinking a group may evolve new norms or ways of thinking in their interactions (Nemeth and Wachtler, 1983).

Given the difficulty of defining groups other than in terms of the influence processes at work or in terms of important characteristics such as shared norms, and having explicitly rejected the reification of the concept, I would prefer to think of groups as an *area of study* whose boundaries are blurred and where not all findings can be immediately or obviously brought together as building blocks towards a unified account or theoretical exposition. Thus we saw that cognitive dissonance theory may lead one to expect that public conformity will lead to private change (Festinger, 1953) and that Moscovici (1980) in exploring minority influences came to the conclusion that private change (conversion) can take place *without* any change at the public level. Whilst these two findings are not irreconcilable, they need different explanations (theories) and they cannot, without further stipulations be fitted into one framework.

Finally, just to keep your adrenalin flowing, I would like to leave you with a paradox. We have seen that small face-to-face groups form spontaneously and hence may be considered an essential part of normal living. Helping an individual to form relationships with others should, therefore, have beneficial consequences; neurotic patients, for instance, may be helped to face their problems and take their first steps back towards normal relationships by the support and sympathy they receive during group psychotherapeutic sessions from others, similarly afflicted. Well known, too, are the methods of groups such as Alcoholics Anonymous: alcoholics, wishing to shake off their dependence on drink, can meet others who have faced the same problems and they can unburden themselves in talking to them; furthermore, they will be supported in their endeavour to stop drinking by a small group of helpers who are available to them on request at any time of day or night. Membership of a group of 'weight watchers' similarly gives an individual the moral strength to abstain from excessive eating.

Studies from industry show that labour turnover is often particularly high in the first weeks of employment. This may be due to a variety of factors, but firms which have made special efforts to integrate newcomers into their organization and into their work-groups find that they can considerably reduce the numbers of those who leave (and hence not only make savings on the cost of recruitment and training but increase the satisfaction of individual staff members who succeed in their jobs rather than leave). Of course, we need to appreciate that such studies were undertaken during periods of full employment and today there may be much stronger initial motivation to stick with a job.

But, and here is the paradox, the group may also be viewed as the *cause* of stress or mental illness. A particular school of psychiatry (for instance, Laing, 1970) thinks of mental illness not as something which is 'located' in the individual; rather the origins of mental illness are seen as the result of faulty interactions in the patient's primary groups, particularly in the family. This may be precisely because it is so difficult for some individuals to seek a way out by leaving the family and its tangled web: we may be eternally attracted by those who destroy us.

SECTION II

Group Membership and Social Control: From Persuasion to Coercion

The fact that we are affected by those with whom we interact has inevitably led to the *use of group situations as potent forms of social control and social change*.

Such attempts to deliberately change the attitudes or the behaviour of group members will be the focus of this second section, in contrast to the first where we were concerned to establish through what processes and in what circumstances members of a group, or of subgroups such as minorities and majorities, influence each other. Attempts to change people raise serious questions.

First of all, there are scientific questions concerned with establishing which measures, if any, are effective in changing people in given contexts.

Secondly, the very research process through which the above questions might be answered may be fraught with ethical problems; for instance, people may be put under great stress in order to observe whether they have a breaking point.

And thirdly, assuming that we have confidence in the validity of the scientific findings, there are ethical issues in implementing them. In particular, even if attempts at changing people stem from benevolent intentions, great care needs to be taken as even good intentions do not necessarily result in beneficial outcomes. Change-agents, that is, people such as politicians, teachers, family planning advisors, health educators, agricultural extension officers and social workers should therefore repeatedly question their motives and implicit or explicit value judgements, their relationship to those they seek to influence as well as their methods (even though, as we shall see, change-agents often tend to be less effective than they hope to be in achieving their goals).

In this section we shall be concerned with these three sets of questions in reviewing a very wide range of topics which illustrate attempts to influence and control other people. We shall be ranging from psychological processes such as persuasion, group decision-making and leadership at the more 'acceptable' end of this continuum to processes such as indoctrination, 'brainwashing' and the application of physical as well as psychological pressures in a milieu which is controlled by the change-agent.

Persuasion

The study of persuasion, that is of communications which are intended to have a predetermined effect on the audience, has a long history dating from at least the 1940s.

Initially, there was concern about the influence of the mass media on the individual who was viewed as an isolated being in a 'mass society' and as such unable to resist 'propaganda', a view which seemed to be confirmed by the use made of mass media by totalitarian régimes in Europe. But anxiety about propaganda and manipulation was not the only starting point for research into persuasion. Many studies were in fact designed to explore how the mass media could be used to greater effect in advertising, in politics or to put across government policies (particularly during the Second World War) so as to ensure the acceptibility of these policies. Indeed the long-term Yale research programme on Communications was the direct descendant of the research branch of the US War Department's Information and Education Division and Hovland, who headed the Yale programme, had started his experimental work whilst employed by the US War Department where he was concerned with the practical problems of briefing American military personnel. The kind of issue Hovland and other social psychologists studied in the laboratory was the relationship between exposure to presuasive communications and the response of individual members of the audience. They focused on such issues as the structure of a communication (for instance whether it contained both pro and contra arguments), the effects of the perceived trustworthiness and expertise of the communicator (for instance when the same message was attributed to a high or low prestige source), the channels through which the persuasive message reached the individual (whether through the mass media or through interpersonal relationships) and individual differences in 'persuasibility'. My justification for looking at some of the research on persuasion derives from the fact that the notion that isolated individuals in modern 'mass society' were hapless victims of mass communications soon proved to be inaccurate. It became apparent that even in the twentieth century interpersonal influences were an important factor mediating between the persuasive communication and the individual recipient of the message. Attention was first drawn to the impact of personal contacts in a study on voting behaviour carried out at the University of Columbia in 1940 by Lazarsfeld, Berelson and Gaudet (published in 1948). They used a 'panel method' where the same individuals were interviewed during the 1940 American presidential election campaign at monthly intervals between May and November. What emerged from the interviews was the findings that few voters changed their candidate preference and that, when changes did occur, they could not be traced directly to mass media sources but rather seemed to depend on interpersonal influences. These researchers developed the so-called 'two-step flow hypothesis' which suggests that 'the influences stemming from the media first reach "opinion leaders" who, in turn, pass on what they read and hear to those of their everyday associates for whom they are influential' (Katz, 1957, pp. 196—7). The term 'opinion leader' does not refer to a person who holds a formal position but to one who comes to be so described on the basis that others turn to him or her for advice and because in consequence of that he or she becomes influential. The two-step flow hypothesis was refined and extended in successive studies carried out between 1940 and 1955 and these studies pointed to the importance of analysing the individual recipient of influence attempts in the context of both his or her primary groups and the wider social context. Riley and Riley (1959), for instance, traced the evolution of models of the mass media (see Figure 5), starting from the initial simplistic view which assumed the media to be very powerful and the individual to be very weak, to one which took account of the interdependence of the communicator and the recipient of the message and the fact that both were embedded in particular social relationships. This view also finds support from a study by Menzel and Katz (1955) which focused on the way doctors make decisions to adopt new drugs. There were several methodological innovations in this piece of work, the most important being the intro- duction of objective data as a cross-check on subjective accounts of decision-making and the flow of influence. For instance, an audit of pres- criptions on file made it possible to verify the precise date when a doctor first prescribed a particular new drug. Once again, the findings pointed to the way in which interpersonal relations 'intervene' in the communication process. Willingness to adopt a new drug was found to relate to the doctor's position in the social structure of his local medical fraternity. Those doctors who were regarded as opinion leaders were most apt to be influenced by information acquired through journal articles or attendance at professional meetings, a finding which confirms the hypothesis of a two-step flow of communications: the doctors who served as a reference group for their colleagues exposed themselves to more information. Conversely, doctors who were isolated from their professional colleagues relied more on commercial sources — direct-mail advertisements from

(a) Over-simplified view: mass society thesis
SOURCE: Secord and Backman (1964 p. 197)

(b) Inclusion of reference groups
SOURCE: Riley and Riley (1959 p. 553)

(c) Contemporary approach: communication in a social system
SOURCE: Riley and Riley (1959 p. 577)

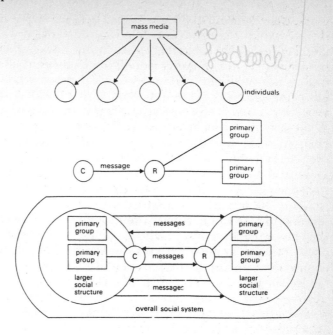

FIGURE 5. Changing sociological models of the communication process

pharmaceutical companies or visits from representatives of drug firms — to learn about new drugs.

Not all aspects of the findings, however, were in keeping with predictions from the original model. Instead of finding that rank-and-file members were influenced by opinion leaders who in turn were influenced by the mass media, Menzel and Katz uncovered a more complex process: '. . . The opinion leaders may themselves turn to colleagues of even higher status and . . . it may take three or four steps . . . rather than two, before a level of leadership is reached where dependence on personal contacts is markedly decreased' (pp. 342–3). The authors therefore proposed a revision of the two-step flow model so as to allow for a multi-step flow of communications.

The importance of group membership in mediating information and 'legitimizing' the adoption of an innovation was also demonstrated in another study which focused on the use of a new hybrid seed-corn. Here, however, the farming community was conservative and traditional and hence those who were well integrated into their local network were least likely to try out the new seed-corn (Rogers, 1962).

Since in this section we are discussing how knowledge about group relationships can and has been used we need to ask ourselves how the insights derived from the above studies help or hinder us in influencing other people. First of all, we need to realize that the *transmission* of information (news, views or advice), whether by personal contacts or by the mass media) does not ensure influence over an audience. How a communication is evaluated, adopted, rejected or modified depends, as the studies of the doctors and the farmers showed, on how well it fits in with the attitudes and expectations of the audience and how the recipients of the information relate to a relevant reference group. To introduce, for instance, an agricultural innovation or a programme of birthcontrol or advocate a no-smoking policy requires much thought on how to communicate the advocated practice, through what combination of change-agent and media, and how to involve the group members in the process of change. Even when a program has utilized available knowledge, many apparently useful or beneficial practices fail to be adopted. Whilst one may regret this in some cases, in other circumstances one may be glad to point to the resilience of people when they are shielded by group membership from influence attempts from outside their own social contexts. Although mass media and interpersonal influences may counterbalance each other, they can also be combined to devastating effects in totalitarian societies which seek to control all aspects of their citizens' lives. In such societies not only is mass media information controlled and access to other sources prevented (through censorship and restrictions on travel abroad) but social networks are mobilized to support a given official position. Thus compulsory youth movements or compulsory attendance at 'discussion groups' are intended to ensure absorption of and adherence to 'approved' views.

The research on persuasive communications has pointed to the interplay between mass media and interpersonal influence processes. It has thus shown that the original fears about the impact of 'mass society' on helpless isolated individuals in modern society were exaggerated. These fears stemmed from the concerns and analyses of European sociologists in the late nineteenth century who witnessed the transition from traditional peasant communities to modern industrialized societies and hence the break-up of small homogeneous communities and the rise of the urban mass. However, the fact that these changes and population movements did not lead to an atomised society of isolated individuals should not preclude us from understanding the very great influence the mass media can and do have over our thinking, feelings and behaviour. Two points need to be made.

(1) The mass media may be very influential in creating what we have

previously referred to as 'shared social representations' in presenting and interpreting the world to us.

(2) We have seen that opinion leaders tend to be avid consumers of the mass media and, whilst the influence of the mass media may not be directly on the individual but impinge on him or her *via* the group and opinion leader, it can be substantial over a period of time, precisely because the media may create the understanding, the interpretations, the images and myths which become our shared representations, which we absorb and which form the backdrop against which we judge new experiences and events (including attempts at persuasion).

We will need to return to some of the issues raised here in studying attempts at persuasion when we consider later research on *indoctrination* and when we come to discuss the phenomenon of the *crowd*.

In the meantime, however, we shall look at some research on group decision-making which was undertaken in the same period as the early communication studies we have just explored.

Decision making in groups

The first study on decision making which I will consider was carried out by Kurt Lewin, a German-born psychologist who came to the United States in the 1930s. He had a strong interest in applying the findings of social psychological research to social reform and social policy, and he is often quoted as saying 'There is nothing more practical than a good theory'. He was the first to engage in 'action research', that is, research where the researcher intervenes in a situation and then monitors the effects the intervention produced. (This should be contrasted with participant field observation where a researcher takes part in the events he or she observes but without, it is hoped, affecting them by his or her presence.) Lewin founded the *Research Center for Group Dynamics* in 1944 at the Massachusetts Institute of Technology and the *Commission for Community Interrelations* of the American Jewish Congress in 1945. He initiated much research into prejudice, discrimination and intergroup relations, including industrial conflict. Even though he died in 1947, when only in his fifties, he has had a tremendous and continuing influence on social psychology. This can be attributed not only to his ability to test theoretical ideas experimentally and to promote action research but through his students and associates, many of whom became leaders in American social psychology.

One of Lewin's major interests was the study of group dynamics. We will first look at his research on group decision making. As we shall see, he came to think that it is easier to induce social change by involving groups, (a view which is entirely compatible with the findings of those who studied persuasive communications) rather than by persuading individuals directly, and to do so by encouraging group members to discover relevant facts for themselves through discussion with others in the group. He thought of reason as a social value and equated reasoning and democracy because 'it grants to reasoning partners a status of equality' (Lewin, 1948, p. 83).

How did he come to evolve such views? During the Second World War Lewin carried out a series of studies to explore how housewives could be induced to change their food habits such as to drink more milk or give their babies orange juice and codliver oil. In these studies he tested the efficacy of presenting information to group members either through a lecture or through eliciting such information through group discussion, the latter method being singled out for study because of Lewin's profound faith in the virtues of democracy. This study is outlined in Box 6.

Box 6   *'Group decision and social change' (Lewin, 1947).*

One of his studies was carried out in 1943 when the US government was anxious to get housewives to serve cheaper cuts of meat to their families. Two methods were used. Three groups of between thirteen and seventeen Red Cross volunteer housewives attended interesting lectures which linked the problem of nutrition with the war effort, emphasized the vitamin and mineral content of offal and stressed health and economic aspects. The preparation of dishes was described and recipes distributed.

In three other groups, composed of the same kind of people, a nutrition expert introduced the same topic and then let the group members discuss the issues. In such a discussion, the expert helps the group with factual information but refrains from telling people what they should do or think or how to overcome their dislike of offal. At the end of the discussion period, members were asked if they would serve kidneys, hearts and so on during the following week and the same recipes were distributed.

A follow-up showed that only three percent of the women who heard the lectures served one of the meats never served before, whereas after group discussion and decision thirty-two percent reported serving at least one such meal.

How can one explain these effects? One possible explanation is that people tend to resist authoritarian pressures but are willing to accept new ideas from their peers. Perhaps the to and fro of discussion allows people to test the appropriateness of various ideas and gives them the feeling that they have convinced themselves and made their own decisions. This process can generate considerable involvement as contrasted with more passive listening to a lecture.

A second reason for the more ready acceptance of new ideas in the discussion groups in these experiments may be the fact that in these groups each member was asked to make a *decision* about her own intentions. (Such individual decisions may be contrasted with those made by juries or committees who make decisions as group members rather than as individuals. In such situations, discusssions may need to be continued till a *consensus* is reached.)

The issue of the importance of actually making a decision was taken up by Pelz (1958) who demonstrated that two factors were instrumental in bringing about the changed perceptions and intentions of the members of discussion groups.

One, a *shared new group norm* evolved during the discussions and became *apparent* to the participants; and two, the act of *making a decision* of one's own choice, whether privately or publicly, led to the commitment to carry it out.

What are some of the wider implication of these studies? Making a decision may convert something external — the proposal of the discussion leader — into something internal, a conscious choice. With no decision, the suggestion is likely to remain external. Unlike a mere group discussion, a group decision should lead to setting up definite goals for action. These goals my be set up for the group as a whole or by each individual in the group for him or herself. But the group discussion and the communication between members is likely to lead to their involvement with the issue and with the subsequent decision. The group decision, in contrast to the influence of a lecture, thus implies a conscious stand on the part of an individual. Lewin's findings may be compared to those we witnessed in the previous section in that the effects of the media parallel those of the lecture and the discussion groups can be likened to the interaction of the opinion leader with his or her group.

We may or may not agree that it is a good thing that housewives can be led to convince themselves that they contribute to their country's war effort by changing the dietary habits of their families. When we return to the effects of group discussion in a later section, we will see that this same process can be used to achieve results that are morally questionable. Even in Lewin's study, we need to remember that the scene is set by the group leader and that the 'ideal' outcome is predefined by him. The aims are to effect a change in the direction desired by the leader and to make the change acceptable to the participants. Group discussions and group decision making are (in cases such as this) an attempt at social control (or 'social engineering' as Lewin called it approvingly though this phrase has since then acquired undesirable attributes), albeit possibly a more acceptable means of control than issuing and enforcing orders. An alternative to persuading people to change their eating habits would presumably involve rationing and laws against blackmarketeering with punishments meted out to those who break the law. Following on from Lewin, group discussions have been used in factories and have been shown to be effective in getting groups of workers to overcome their resistance to changes in work practices desired by management (for example, see Coch and French, 1948). However, we need to note that such 'participation' by workers is likely to be effective (from the point of view of the management) only if there are no fundamental economic or ideological differences between the workers and the management. Where both management and workers desire the *same* ends, for instance increased productivity, then group discussions and decisions will utilize the workers' knowledge and may enhance their pride and commitment.

You may have your own views as to whether such efforts at making the exercise of authority less autocratic by fostering conditions, through information and discussion, in which the individual and the work-group may identify with the objectives of an organization and participate in the decision making process are an attempt at democratizing decision making at the work place. Some critics hold that this approach is 'manipulative' since, far from lessening managerial control, it may make its exercise more effective because organizational objectives will have been understood and more readily accepted and, hence, control by the managerial hierarchy will also be supported by peer-group pressures.

Group discussions need not merely be a method of engineering consensus (though this is our focus in this section). They also provide the possibility of pooling knowledge and skills in finding solutions to problems (be they design problems in industry or a case conference of social workers). They need not be chaired by someone with a predetermined aim. They can be fairly unstructured as in 'brainstorming' sessions though there is controversy over whether such methods do, in fact, foster creativity. Whilst here I have focused on the effects on members of *making* a decision, individually or as a group, there is also considerable research (and controversy) on how groups *arrive* at their decisions. Is group decision making dependant on the minority stimulating rethinking in the majority? Do groups make more extreme decisions (group polarization) than individuals do on their own, or does the pressure to reach consensus lead decision making groups to overlook important evidence with the result that they produce erroneous or low quality solutions — a phenomenon named 'group think' by Janis (1982). He defines 'group think' as 'a mode of thinking that people engage in when they are deeply involved in a cohesive in-group, when the members' striving for unanimity override their motivation to realistically appraise alternative courses of action' (1982, p. 9). Such groups tend to get locked into a particular decision and suppress attempts to examine the decision by taking into account a wider range of factors. They thus do not produce or evaluate alternative decisions. They value the comfort of consensus and of good interpersonal relationships. However, non-cohesive groups are not necessarily better at making decisions; their members may pull in different directions or have insufficient interest in and commitment to working out a solution to the problem the group needs to make decisions on. Cohesive groups can learn to guard against premature consensus and learn to evaluate alternatives. But there are well-known instances of people shutting their minds to evidence of changes in the environment which require investigation and decisions. Thus it has been shown that neither the attack on the American Fleet at Pearl Harbour (Wohlstetter, 1962) nor the Argentine invasion of the Falklands should have come as a surprise (Franks, 1983).

These two examples from the political sphere have been well documented but if you work in any kind of organization you may be able to think back to decisions taken there which placed too much emphasis on consensus and neglected opposing views or information with the result that these decisions were impracticable or untenable in the long if not the short run.

The emphasis upon groups and the desirability of involving individuals in change has, since Lewin's death, led to such developments as T (for training) groups, later called sensitivity groups. These groups are led by a relatively non-directive but sensitively observing 'trainer' or 'facilitator' with the intention of giving participants insight into their own motivation and behaviour. Indeed it was Lewin who founded the *National Training Laboratories* at Bethel, Maine, where these groups orginated, but he died before the work got into its stride.

Related to these later developments and Lewin's original work there has been in recent years a growth of various self-help movements such as Alcoholics Anonymous and smoking clinics which are intended to help individuals to help themselves. Such self-help groups tend to have predetermined aims (for instance the members of a group of weight-watchers want to shed surplus weight) but membership is voluntary and the individuals joining such groups have themselves taken the initiative in seeking to effect a change in their behaviour or attitudes (though you may feel in the case of groups of weight-watchers that they have been 'manipulated' by the media to think that being slim is important). Such groups, like Lewin's groups, tend to be chaired by an expert who gives advice on diet. Members *decide* publicly on their own targets of weight reduction and it is the approval and support of members which help each individual to reach his or her goal. Whether such group-based methods of self-persuasion can be thought of as aiding personal growth and self-control is a matter of opinion. Many groups have sprung up, not to pursue such specific aims as to control smoking or lose weight, but in a more general quest for a satisfying life. Perhaps such groups thrive particularly in times of cultural change; for instance, in the wake of the women's liberation movement, consciousness raising and assertiveness training groups flourished and other self-help groups also emerged in the 1960s and 1970s. Some people move from one such group experience to the next, from 'encounter groups' to 'primal therapy' to 'transactional analysis' and so on, without apparently finding either salvation or even a modicum of happiness, integrity as a person, or an increase in competence in dealing with everyday life. Others have found satisfaction in developing new insights and guidelines for their lives.

In looking in this section at group decision making we have made reference, albeit more or less in passing, to leaders — discussion leaders, experts, trainers and 'facilitators'. In the next section we shall come to look on such leaders as 'democratic' leaders but, at the same time, we shall see that there are also other types of leaders.

Leadership

The study of leadership has a long history as a research theme and the questions which have been asked about this topic reflect changing interests in social psychology as well as changing perceptions of a leader's role in society. Social scientists tend to define the problems they investigate in terms of the theoretical framework and the empirical traditions in which they work, and, as a consequence, may ignore issues which are of concern either to the public or to social scientists adhering to different schools of thought. If one is interested in personality one may investigate, for instance, why some people are more susceptible than others to persuasive communications. On the other hand, if one starts from the point of view that the social context is likely to predominate over personality and attitudes or individual values, one will study the impact of different situations on people's readiness to adopt advocated opinions. Thus, the research design may predetermine the findings by precluding certain factors from consideration. However, there is another potential source of bias. Social scientists may research problems very much in the way in which have been presented to them by those who pay for the research. Whilst this is a quite general point, it is particularly relevant to the study of human relations in industry which has been largely financed by management or institutions supported by the government rather than by trade unions. One may well speculate as to the questions trade unions would have posed had they thought of financing research. It is also a pertinent comment on research on leadership which has often been commissioned and financed by military authorities and by managements. Research is not invalidated because it is sponsored but one ought to be aware that such sponsorship may produce a limited range of research questions and that other aspects may remain obscure and unresearched.

Early studies of leadership

Early work on leadership attempted to identify the personality characteristics which successful leaders have in common but such research invariably showed that successful leaders could have widely different traits and attributes. Just think of, say, a military commander and an abbess in charge of a convent; or the leader of an expedition bent on conquering an unclimbed mountain peak and a leader of a discusssion group. All these are leaders but they may need quite different personalities, aptitudes or skills. The point to note is not that personal qualities and relevant knowledge are unimportant but that it has proved impossible to make a list of attributes or traits which fits a wide range of leaders without considering these leadership qualities *in relation to the situations and the problems to be faced by the membership of the group in question*. Nevertheless, as we shall see, 'personality' in various guises has come to the fore from time to time in leadership research.

Leadership style

Leaving the focus on personality aside we can turn to a pioneering study of leadership which was carried out by Lewin and his colleagues (Lewin *et al.*, 1939) who examined not so much a leader's personality as his or her *leadership style*. For Lewin, the crucial determinant of group atmosphere lies in leadership and the style adopted by the leader. His research is described in Box 7.

Box 7   *Research on leadership style (Lewin et al., 1939).*

Lewin, as a refugee from totalitarianism, was concerned to establish the superiority the 'democratic' method of leadership. To this end he arranged for three groups of boys to join a club to make models after school hours. One group was led by an 'autocratic' leader who issued orders; the second one was led by a 'democratic' leader who got the children to discuss what they wanted to do and how to achieve their objectives; the final group worked with a 'laissez-faire' leader who was present but did not initiate any action. The leaders for these groups were not chosen by dint of their 'democratic' or 'autocratic' or 'laissez-faire' personalities. They acted the way they did because Lewin told them to present a particular *leadership style* to their groups.

  The 'democratic' group always met two days before the 'autocratic' group. The 'democratic' group chose its activities freely and whatever they had *chosen* to do, the 'autocratic' and 'laissez-faire' groups were then *told* to do. In this way there would be a basis for comparing the 'output' of the children as well as their experience and behaviour.

Lewin found that the 'productivity' of the first two groups was quite comparable but the children in the 'autocratic' group were dissatisfied and some of them became aggressive (to each other rather than the leader) and resentful, whilst others retreated into apathy. In the 'democratic' group there was a good deal of cooperation among the children and they enjoyed the group. The 'laissez-faire' group was neither very productive nor particularly satisfied. Lewin subsequently told the leaders to change their original style and it was again the style which affected the outcome in the various groups. The fact that a leader can be instructed to adopt a particular style implies that managers or officers or other leaders can be helped, through training, to adopt a style which corresponds to the expectations of their group members. Lewin also changed two of the most aggressive children from the 'autocratic' to the 'democratic' group where they quickly became cooperative members who enjoyed the after school clubs. The lesson here is, as the British Army has so graphically expressed it long before these studies took place: there are no bad soldiers, only bad officers.

These results, of course, need to be understood in the context of the social climate in which they took place, a context which favoured democracy above autocracy. If these experiments could have been carried out in Nazi Germany the result might well have shown that the children were more at ease in the 'autocratic' group. This reservation on the general validity of these studies makes a very important point — that individuals, their groups and leaders can only be understood in the context of the wider society of which they form a part. School clubs, the army, industrial or any other kind of organizations cannot, ultimately, be studied as if they were closed systems. The style of leadership which is acceptable (and hence, other things being equal, effective) is intimately bound up with the norms prevalent in the wider society. The participants in organizations occupy roles outside the organizations which serve as a basis for their level of expectations within the organization and for the social comparison processes which determine their perception of the equity or inequity of any transaction within the organization.

Selection of army officers

Lewin's research had no direct influence on the changes which took place in the British Army's methods of selecting its officers during the Second World War but the changes described below developed out of similar concerns.

In the British Army, officers used to have to buy their commissions but even when this practice was stopped they tended still to be recruited from the public schools. A radical change took place during the Second World

War when the supply of potential officers from such a narrow stratum of society proved insufficient in both quantity and quality. With the help of psychiatrists and psychologists new methods of selection were developed. In addition to being interviewed by psychiatrists and taking batteries of psychological tests (to ensure that these potential officers were 'normal'), candidates were put into groups which faced the kind of problems junior officers might have to deal with. These situations required cooperation but there were no obvious solutions; indeed some had no solution which increased the stressfulness of the situation. What mattered to the selectors was not so much the quality of the ideas individuals put forward but how they related to other people in the group, whether a person's suggestions were adopted by the other group members and carried out or whether an individual opted out or perhaps became inflexible when frustrated.

These selection procedures were so successful that they are essentially still in operation and are, in a modified version, also used for the selection of civil service administrative trainees (the 'countryhouse method') and for management trainees.

The army candidates so selected did well in their officer training courses and subsequently in the field. The method was also more acceptable to potential candidates and appeared to be more 'democratic' than selection by interview. One of those who participated in developing these group-based selection methods was W.R. Bion who later became a pioneer of group psychotherapy (Bion, 1961).

Stemming in part from these group-based methods of selection, research on leadership switched in the 1950s from the identification of personality characteristics to *situational determinants* of leadership effectiveness. The main thrust of this approach was to highlight the dependence of the leader upon his or her group. This is virtually the opposite of the approach which locates the leader's power within his or her personality. The situational approach equates the leader's status with his or her ability to command liking from the group and deal with its immediate problems. In time, researchers became aware of the limitations of this view, and adopted, as we shall see, a perspective on leadership which looked on it as a complex social process, a transaction or exchange among members of a group. This new perspective or model posited that the nature of the task, the structure of the group and the expectations and perceptions of the followers all influence the process of leadership.

Leadership in industry

During the 1950s and early 1960s there was still considerable interest in the notion of leadership style, particularly in the effects a supervisor's or manager's leadership style had on those they organized and supervised. Sayles (1966) reviewed both experimental and survey studies on styles of leadership. He found the emerging picture inconsistent; no superiority of one style over another was demonstrated in the *experimental studies* of supervisors though *survey studies* revealed the greater acceptability and productivity of 'democratic' over 'autocratic' leadership. Sayles contends that the tasks in the experimental studies were of such a boring and limited nature (and in that, of course, they resembled many industrial tasks) that people did not become involved and variations in leadership style had relatively little impact. Sayles makes the point that supervisors who use a 'democratic' leadership style probably also differ in other ways from their more 'autocratic' colleagues. He thinks the former are more likely to be intelligent (since research on the 'authoritarian personality' (Adorno *et al.*, 1950) has shown a correlation between low intelligence and high scores on scales which indicate authoritarian attitudes). If 'democratic' supervisors are more intelligent then, clearly, they can deal better with both production difficulties (which may affect wages) and with 'human relations' problems. It seems very obvious that a supervisor needs to address both these issues and, yet, industrial social psychology in the 1950s and 1960s seemed to be almost wholly preoccupied with the notion that managers need to be 'people-centred' rather than 'task-centred' (and this stance of course, was a reaction to the previous over-emphasis on technical aspects of the supervisor's job).

In the 1960s, in parallel with the above emphases, there was again a resurgence of interest in the personality characteristics of the leader though the model adopted was more sophisticated than earlier approaches. Fiedler (1967, 1968, 1971) was initially interested in the inclination of the leader to distinguish between his most and least prefered co-worker (LPC). His researches showed that leaders who see their LPC in a relatively favourable light tend to be more accepting, permissive, considerate and 'person-oriented' in their relations with group members. The person who sees his most and least preferred co-worker as quite different, and the latter in an unfavourable light, tends to be directive, controlling, 'task-oriented' and dominant in his interactions. Fiedler then developed (and tested in several countries and in different organizational contexts) his *contingency model* for the analysis of leadership effectiveness. He sees the effectiveness of leaders as *contingent* on the fit between their personal qualities and their leadership style (whether 'relationship-oriented' or 'task-oriented') on the one hand and the needs of the situation on the other. Thus, his model predicts varying levels of effectiveness for different combinations of leader and situational characteristics. Fiedler distinguishes three situational variables which influence the leader role:

1 the quality of leader—member relations, that is, the extent to which the leader has the confidence of his or her group and, more generally, the psychological climate of the group;
2 the task structure, that is, the complexity and clarity of the task and the number of solutions which are possible: the more unstructured

the task, the more the leader must inspire and motivate people rather than rely on backing by *his* or *her* superiors;

3 the position power of the leader, that is, the power inherent in his or her position, the rewards and punishments at his or her disposal and the organizational support on which he or she can depend.

Fiedler predicted that the managing, controlling leaders perform most effectively either in very favourable or in very unfavourable situations. Considerate, permissive leaders obtain optimal group performance under situations intermediate in favourableness such as where the leader is liked but has an ambiguous unstructured task and must therefore draw on the knowledge and cooperation of group members. Fiedler re-analysed data from his earlier research and also carried out a major experiment to test his model. Both yielded considerable support for this theory. Fiedler's data thus support the idea that leadership effectiveness depends not only on the characteristics of the leadership style and the personal attributes of the leader (such as the ability to make discriminating judgements of group members) but on their *relevance* to the needs of the particular situation. Situational factors, such as the task structure, the degree of power the leader has, and the leader—member relations, affect what form of leadership ('permissive' or 'autocratic', 'people-' or 'task-centred') is likely to be effective. Fiedler's findings (that organizational structure or technology — the task structure — define the appropriate personal style) parallel the conclusions drawn from the work of Woodward (1965).

Joan Woodward showed, by comparing eighty firms variously engaged in unit or small batch, large batch or mass, and flow production that the technology of manufacture influences the organizational structure of the firm and that the structure, in turn, profoundly affects the relationships between managers, supervisors and workers. She found in her study that the technology of production influences such aspects of management as the degree of centralization of decision-making, the degree to which standard procedures can be established, the extent to which specialist services are developed and the ratio of managers to workers and the style of management.

Trist and his fellow workers (Trist *et al.*, 1963) at the Tavistock Istitute of Human Relations took a somewhat different line. They showed that one need not take a technological system of production as 'given' in a situation from which then follow certain organizational consequences and effects on relationships at work. When a new technological system of coal-mining (the so called long—wall method) was introduced, they were able to design work practices which did not disrupt the group cohesion (which is a feature of mining work) and which continued to meet the social and psychological needs of the miners and yet achieve superior economic results. Thus both Woodward and Trist and his colleagues (and others, too) found, like Fiedler, that it is not very useful to study leadership (or management) except in relation to other aspects of a situation.

Fiedler's 'theory of leadership effectiveness' provides a complex and elegant model embodying both *situational* variables such as task structure and power position and *psychological* variables such as the leader's ability to make discriminating assessments of fellow-workers as part of the leader's style. Fiedler, incidentally, thinks of a person's leadership style as a relatively stable personality attribute whereas earlier work by Lewin and his colleagues (Lewin *et al.*, 1939) suggested that a leader can be taught to adopt a new style though this need not necessarily imply a change in outlook and deeply held attitudes. Some people may well use a leadership style which is not a true expression of their basic attitudes or their implicit views of human nature but is a 'copy' of the models of leadership style they themselves have been exposed to or which corresponds to the style of colleagues or the firm's policies. Whether or not changing one's style is easy or possible depends, therefore, on a variety of antecedent as well as current factors. Fiedler, as we have seen, is interested in exploring whether different leadership styles are appropriate for different situations. In other words, he is interested in the 'fit' between the psychological and situational variables. Far from suggesting, however, that leaders should be encouraged to change their style of management to fit the situation, Fiedler (1965) suggests that we must learn how to 'engineer' the job to fit the leadership style and the needs of managers who happen to be available. His grounds for stating this are that intelligent and technically competent people are in short supply, that training is costly and time-consuming whilst a little thought would allow one to place people into situations compatible with their 'natural' leadership style. Selectively used, this approach might well be fruitful in some situations. It should be possible, at times at any rate, to change both task structures (as Trist *et al.* did) and the power position of the leader. The third situational variable, that of the quality of the group—leader relationships, cannot be easily manipulated, or indeed, precisely operationalized and assessed. It might itself, of course, be influenced, if not in the short run then in the long run, by the leader's style. The perception of the leader's legitimacy will be influenced by the extent to which he or she meets the normative expectations of his or her co-workers, including their expectations concerning the leader's competence to meet their task or socio-emotional needs. The expectations of the group members as to their preferred style of leadership mesh, probably, with the task structure and their own motivation. An individual will 'judge' a leader's actions and motives in accordance with his or her own needs for job satisfaction and/or other rewards, such as bonus payments which may depend on the organizational ability of the leader/manager.

Interestingly and rather surprisingly in view of the fact that he earlier thought of a leader's style as a relatively stable attribute, Fiedler in a later paper (1972) suggests that leaders themselves have varying needs and goals and they might, therefore, vary their behaviour and adapt to the situation in which they find themselves. 'Controlling' leaders might become 'relationship orientated' and leaders who employ a 'permissive' style might use a 'controlling' style when they operate in situations which make a different approach more effective or which allow the satisfaction of needs which are of only secondary importance in other situations.

Fiedler, therefore, seems to be suggesting a new element of indeterminacy in his model. Although he specifies what he considers to be the relevant inputs in the leadership situation, he appears to be qualifying the nature of these 'givens'. None remains absolute and he describes a truly interactive process in which both leaders and led may adapt, and task and power structures can also be changed. This, of course, means that it is impossible to predict the directions in which the system might move — at least, in terms of this particular analytic framework. If Fiedler's suggestion that the situation can be 'engineered' to fit the leader and his or her style of leadership is feasible then, equally, it should be possible to 'engineer' situations to fit the needs and capacities of other participants in the interests of personal satisfaction as well as efficiency or productivity. Fiedler, however, is concerned with leader effectiveness (in getting the job done). Unlike Lewin, he does not address himself to the question of whether a particular style of leadership also aids the satisfaction of co-workers' needs nor does he concern himself explicitly with the perception of the leader by the followers. I think this imbalance in the model, or, rather, the neglect of the variable of reciprocal perceptions, is probably due to the assumptions made in the model that a leader tends to have a formal position which provides him with legitimacy and varying degrees of power (and hence the perceptions of the followers do not matter as much as the leader's skill in assessing co-workers). This is often the case and a relevant starting point to take in writing about leadership effectiveness, but leaders can be challenged, deposed or ignored (in organizations as well as everywhere else) and new leaders may emerge to deal with new situations or to fill needs not met by the former leaders. It is, of course, also true that, when a leader has come to the fore, say, in an unofficial strike, he or she will try, if the problem is not quickly solved, to create an aura of legitimacy by getting explicit support from followers for carrying on the struggle. Such 'unofficial' leaders gain support when they meet the needs of their followers better than 'official' leaders, be they managers or trade union leaders. Incidentally, in laboratory experiments it has been found that elected, as opposed to appointed, leaders feel freer to disagree with their group members (Hollander and Julian, 1970). This might suggest that the elected members were more secure in their status (at least for the time being).

The style of leadership leaders adopt may vary with their perceptions of the psychological situation in which they find themselves and it is, therefore, not necessarily a stable personality characteristic. Thus an 'autocratic' field commander of a guerilla force may eventually become a 'democratic' and constitutional head of his country. Whether or not leadership style is a personality characteristic, control (or leadership) in organizations is based both on power (inherent in a particular position) and on legitimating approval from subordinates, peers and superiors and hence tends to conform broadly to commonly held norms and expectations on how such authority is to be exercised. The leader is part of this context, not outside it.

Effective leadership, then, depends on successful transactions between the leaders and the led and, in part, this process depends on how they perceive each other. Arising from the success of Japanese industry simple-minded questions are often asked as to whether Japanese managers are 'better' than their American or European counterparts. Posing such question implies the erroneous notion that leadership can be defined in a culture free manner. Japanese styles of management are intimately linked to the social structure of their society and the attitudes and expectations of the work force in their own country. If Japanese methods were imposed on people in other countries, they might be unacceptable, misperceived, misjudged and hence ineffective. Smith (1984) reviews studies of Japanese-owned firms in the United States and Europe and is able to show that in fact not all the distinctive qualities of Japanese work organization and management style are introduced or imposed by the Japanese when operating in different cultural contexts.

Communication networks and leadership

From a quite different line of research we have some evidence which supports the idea that leadership is not an inborn personality charac- teristic. These studies show that, when people are put into positions where the group needs to depend on their efforts, they tend to rise to the challenge and behave as leaders and are also recognized by others as such.

These findings derive from studies in which a communication network is imposed on experimental groups. Left to their own devices groups naturally evolve their own communication structures. Research on imposed structures (e.g. Leavitt, 1951) has tried to establish whether given communication networks facilitate or hinder the performance of a group of four or five people in the completion of a task. These researchers showed that for simple tasks basically involving the assembly of information held by different members of the group, the networks with a *central* person (wheel, Y and chain in Figure 6) proved most effective (in that order). For the solution of complex problems, the more diffuse net- works of the circle groups proved faster and the all-channel commu- nication network (Davis and Hornseth, 1967), reproduced in Figure 7, proved most effective (and superior to individuals solving the same problems on their own). It is likely that the all-channel network's superiority was due to its openness and flexibility which enabled some members to play a more prominent part and to by-pass others who were less able to cope with the task at hand. By contrast, the extent to which alternative structures can emerge in a wheel network is minimal.

These studies are mentioned here in our review of leadership because they provided some interesting findings concerning the central role. Those people who by chance held central positions in the network tended to evolve as decision makers and were generally judged to be leaders by the other group members. In comparison with people in peripheral positions they tended to send more messages, to solve problems more quickly, to make fewer errors and to be more satisfied with group and personal efforts. In other words, it would appear that it was primarily the position in the network and not 'personality' which led to the assumption of the leadership role.

Berkowitz (1956) took these studies further in order to examine the interaction between personality characteristics and the central role. He used problems which had also been used by other experimenters and a Y network composed of four people (figure 8). This study is described in Box 8.

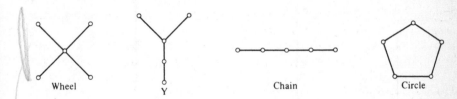

FIGURE 6.   *Five person networks*

FIGURE 7.   *All-Channel network*

FIGURE 8.   *Four person Y network*
SOURCE: Davis (1969)

Box 8   Personality and behaviour in central and peripheral roles
(Berkowitz, 1956).

In advance of the problem solving sessions Berkowitz tested his subjects for certain personality characteristics which he designated as 'high-ascendant', 'low-ascendant' and 'moderately-ascendant'.

In half his experimental groups a high-ascendant person occupied the central position, in the other half a low-ascendant person occupied the central position. The resulting messages were coded as 'relaying' information received from others (passive behaviour) or as 'initiating' communications such as proposing solutions or asking for further information (active behaviour).

The results indicated that both personality and role requirements influenced behaviour. For instance, in the *peripheral* positions, the low-ascendant subjects sent a significantly higher percentage of information — relaying messages than did the high-ascendant subjects when occupying these same peripheral positions.

More interesting, however, is the *change* in the behaviour of low-ascendant subjects when they occupied the central positions. Over time they decreased in passivity and came to behave like high-ascendant subjects in the central position.

In other words, if one can generalize from a laboratory experiment to the 'real' world, people can come to respond to the demands of a situation and, in the present case, behave like leaders even though, initially, they did not appear to have the psychological attributes ('high ascendancy') of a leader. This does not, of course, imply that *any* person can fill *any* role but that the demand characteristics of the role may elicit hidden talents.

More generally, these studies suggest that for simple or routine problems and decisions an explicit communication structure with a central person (such as a charge-hand or supervisor in an industrial organization) is likely to be effective. For creative or complex problems (such as may be faced by more senior management) the more open networks seem to give better results in terms of the quality of the solutions produced and in terms of personal satisfaction.

These studies all show the importance of having relevant information in order to arrive at the solution of problems. It is perhaps not entirely accidental, therefore, that many relatively lowly placed executives or supervisors can often be seen to display a marked tendency to hoard such information as they have and keep it from others so that those who work with them have to appeal to them for advice, guidance, instructions or decisions. Such leaders tend to cling to their central positions and may be very autocratic in their relationships. The networks of more democratic leaders are more likely to be of the all-channel variety.

Leadership and the influence of the minority

How does our exploration of leadership link to the topics discussed in Section I? There, in studying interactions of people and putting forward explanations of the social influence processes at work in groups, I have not referred to leadership as the authors I reviewed have not done so either. In that earlier section we were concerned mainly with *spontaneously* occurring influence processes between individuals or between minorities and majorities, albeit in settings created by the experimenter who could be equated with the leader. In particular, you may think that the experimenter, described as an 'authority figure' by Milgram when conducting his experiments on obedience corresponds to our notion of a leader. He had, at any rate in the eyes of his subjects, power and status and he exerted influence on the subjects the extent of which varied according to the conditions of each experiment.

You can also think back to the discussion of the notion of 'behavioural style' put forward by Moscovici and his co-workers. Consistency, investment and autonomy which were mentioned there as essential characteristics of a minority, intent on influencing a majority, may well also denote a leadership style.

We have also referred to opinion leaders when we discussed the transmission and spread of information or opinions. As you may remember, opinion leaders were described as informal leaders who mediate information from the media to those who look up to them as 'opinion leaders' in a particular field of knowledge, be that politics, fashion, medical innovation or anything else. They are leaders and have influence not by virtue of their formal position, authority or power but by virtue of their perceived expertise and trustworthiness. Thus, leaders may have influence without a formal platform and, conversely, formal 'leaders' can be without influence if their 'followers' turn elsewhere for guidance or the satisfaction of their needs.

The prestige of the leaders and hence the extent of their influence is something which does not derive solely or even mainly from their formal position; it is something which accrues to them over time. Once they have gained the trust and respect of those they interact with they can, and are sometimes expected to, deviate from the norms of the group. Leaders have acquired, as Hollander (1958) termed it, 'idiosyncrasy credit' and this enables them to innovate and move the group towards decisions or innovations which might not previously have been acceptable to its members. In fact, the leader becomes a minority and, where a leader is concerned with changing people, as in Lewin's discussion groups, he or she is at the outset always in a minority.

We have earlier discussed the influence a minority may have on the majority in a group. Are Moscovici's ideas and findings concerning the importance of the behavioural style of the minority compatible with Hollander's view? Both Moscovici and Hollander agree that a minority can influence those in the majority but they differ in explaining how such influence is achieved. Hollander proposes that a group member holding a minority position must conform initially to the majority position and prove himself competent before being allowed by others in the group to deviate and innovate without losing his influence. By contrast Moscovici and Faucheux (1972) suggest that the minority must consistently and resolutely *not* conform from the outset and that the minority's behavioural style is the source of its influence. Bray *et al.* (1982) were intrigued by these discrepancies between the two models and set up two experiments to see whether they could obtain evidence which would allow them to decide which of these models of minority influence is better supported. Their study is described in Box 9.

Box 9   *'Social influence by group members with minority opinions: A comparison of Hollander and Moscovici', Bray et al., 1982*

In their first experiment four-person male groups discussed three opinion issues that were selected to permit a single confederate to argue for the minority position. In the Hollander strategy the confederate argued the minority position only on the last issue, whereas in the Moscovici strategy he argued it on every issue. The second experiment followed the same procedure except that both male and female subjects were tested and groups contained six members with two confederates. Bray and his colleagues found that both the Hollander and Moscovici models were supported in that the opinions of subjects were influenced significantly when compared to those of controls individuals who did not receive any influence attempt. However, the Hollander model produced influence with only one person deviating from the majority, while the Moscovici model required a minority of at least two people. There were also sex differences: with male subjects, Hollander's model produced significantly greater influence than Moscovici's model; for female groups, whilst overall they were less influenced than the male groups, both models achieved similar degrees of influence.

These experiments, whilst not conclusive, suggest that in order to achieve or retain influence a single person who deviates from the group's position may need to adopt a strategy which is different from that which is effective for a minority of two.

In other words, the influence processes between a group and its leader, even though he or she has begun to deviate from group norms and in that sense has become a minority, seem to be different from those which operate between a small minority and a larger majority.

Finally, then, we have seen in this section that, in order to understand the phenomenon of leadership, we need to consider, as so often in social psychology, the interaction of several factors: the immediate situational context, the wider society and culture, and individual differences (in this case in leadership style and relevant knowledge).

Coercion: Manipulating group membership

At the beginning of this section I pointed out that, in considering deliberate influence attempts, we would be ranging from relatively innocuous or even benign influence processes to those which pose more of a threat to the individual. These latter processes can be labelled as coercion but it is as well to point out again that we are discussing a continuum of influence processes rather than a radical dichotomy between 'acceptable' and 'unacceptable' influence attempts. Nevertheless, coercion can be distinguished from persuasion or leadership or group pressures toward conformity chiefly in terms of the amount and type of pressure being exerted and in the intentions of the influence agent. The term coercion refers to situations where the influence agent has obtained considerable control over the physical as well as the psychological environment of the victim — and I choose this word deliberately. Manipulating the environment is, of course, often done with intentions and effects generally thought to be beneficial. A teacher may create a physical and psychological environment in which children are keen to explore and learn. The layout of a housing estate can be planned so as to facilitate social contacts among the residents and hence create a feeling of neighbourliness and of belonging to a community (Gans, 1972) or to reduce vandalism (Newman, 1972). Similarly the design of a psychiatric ward (Osmond, 1957) may aid interaction among patients and staff and reduce isolation and loneliness. Or, as Deutsch and Collins (1951) and others have shown, enabling black and white residents on a housing estate to make contact with each other may lead to a reduction in racial prejudice. The 'busing' of children in the United States to schools in other areas so that different racial groups meet and mix with each other is also intended to reduce racial antagonisms (though this measure has lead to other problems such as children having no friends in their own locality and it has been largely abandoned). Such manipulations of the environment, however, tend to affect only some aspects of everyday life. Here we will now consider the more overwhelming effects of pervasive environmental control, where the coercive agent attempts to gain control of the 'total milieu' of those to be influenced. We shall see, too, that group membership is again an important context in facilitating or hindering the agent's exercise of coercive powers.

Total institutions

The first study of 'milieu control' I want to consider here addresses itself to the situation in which hospitalized mental patients may find themselves. Goffman coined the word 'total institutions' to describe such all-embracing environments. He defines them 'as a place of residence and work where a large number of like-situated individuals, cut off from the wider society for an appreciable period of time, together lead an enclosed, formally administered round of life' (Goffman 1968, p. 11).

Normally, people live in one place, work somewhere else, seek leisure somewhere else again and mix with a range of people. The central feature of total institutions can be described as a breakdown of the barriers ordinarily separating these three spheres of life. *Inmates* of total institutions (such as officer cadets, nuns, children at boarding school, prisoners or patients in mental hospitals) typically have only restricted contact with the world outside; the *staff* may be socially integrated with their wider society but the extent to which they may be so integrated and hence influenced by the mores and values of the community outside their institution may depend on their geographical situation on the one hand and, on the other, on how far they feel that outsiders understand and are sympathetic to their professional roles and responsibilities.

A total institution affords the possibility of a high level of psychological control over its inmates since the institution controls all aspects of their lives. The inmates lack access to outside contacts, roles or reference groups. However, the fact that total institutions encompass all aspects of a person's life need not in itself lead to autocratic or coercive behaviour on the part of the staff. A total institution such as a *kibbutz* or commune may be egalitarian and democratic (though because of the relative lack of outside contacts, may yet achieve great similarity in views and behaviour among its members). Whether membership is voluntary or involuntary also need not be crucial to the effect of the influence of the staff (or existing members) on new entrants. According to Goffman the basis of the coercive power of the staff is the emphasis on and institutional arrangements made for creating and maintaining *inequality* and *social distance* between inmates and staff. This power can be used to rob individuals of normal supports to their conceptions of their own selves. Thus Goffman describes how on admission patients are stripped of their 'identity kit' in that they may not be allowed to retain their personal possessions, wear their own clothes or even keep their own dentures. They may be referred to by a number rather than by name (and in Nazi concentration camps had this number stenciled permanently on the wrist). The inmates, according to Goffman, may be systematically degraded and mortified through the conditions of their physical environment as well as through the behaviour of the staff and they may be deprived not only of freedom but of all discretion in structuring their daily life — when to eat, sleep, go to the lavatory, or what to work at, or what activities to engage in apart from work. In these circumstances it is, according to Goffman, well nigh impossible for the inmate to maintain his or her previous self since the self, the individual's personality, is a 'persona' or mask donned for a particular audience and the result of the interaction of a performance with a specific audience: 'A correctly staged and performed scene leads the audience to impute a self to a performed character, but this imputation — the self — is a product of a scene that comes off, it is not a cause of it (Goffman, 1971, p. 245).

This description of the self as a transient enactment of a role is, of course, not universally accepted. Goffman, however, declares that robbing people of the props to their identity is indeed to rob them of their identity. He envisages the ensuing restructuring of the self or identity as if this new self were an artificial graft, unrelated to the individual's previous personality and he declares that 'the self is not a property of the person to whom it is attributed, but dwells rather in the pattern of social control' and that the 'institutional arrangement does not so much support the self as constitute it' (Goffman, 1968, p. 154). If the latter statement were taken to be literally true then one would not expect patients to adapt in individual and diverse ways to the demands of the social situation in which they find themselves. Goffman himself describes in one of the essays ('The underlife of a public institution') in his book *Asylum* (1968) 'ways of making out in a mental hospital'. Some patients, he claims, withdraw from the situation into themselves, others make the institution their home to the extent that they do not wish to leave it and yet others become converts to the views the staff have of them. Such variation in the perception of the response to the same demands can only be explained in terms of the individual's personality, albeit diminished and robbed of its customary supports as it may be in particular institutional contexts.

Whilst one may not wish wholly to accept Goffman's sociological version of personality, one has to recognize his importance in pointing to situationally determined changes in personality or behaviour. He states quite explicitly that hospitalization (or admission to prison or some other total institution) is such a traumatic event and entails such a fundamental change in a patient's life that the effect of these changes can be studied by assuming that all patients, irrespective of symptoms or diagnosis, are faced by similar circumstances and react to them in similar ways. He writes:

> It is a tribute to the power of social forces that the uniform status of mental patient cannot only assure an aggregate of persons a common fate and eventually, because of this, a common character, but that this social reworking can be done upon what is perhaps the most obstinate diversity of

human materials that can be brought together by society. (Goffman 1968, p. 121).

One must not lose sight of the fact that the staff, too, are affected by those with whom they are in contact. On joining an institution they are being socialized into their roles by explicit instruction and training as well as by the example set by the existing staff. But one may well wonder how far the agents of control are themselves controlled by their inferiors: a prison warder, say, to have a quiet life needs to reach a *modus vivendi* with his or her charges.

Goffman, then, by taking situational variables as his only significant influences on personality and behaviour takes an extreme stand we need not share. But his views on total institutions and on personality serve as a strident and dramatic lead-in to the discussion of other coercive situations.

Thought reform

The term thought reform is a translation of the Chinese word which describes the psychological techniques used by the Chinese communists to effect changes in political views and in self-concept. These techniques are also sometimes referred to as brainwashing but this seems an emotive as well as a meaningless term if it is intended to imply that the human mind can be wiped clean like a slate and a new start be made.

I should like to discuss Chinese thought reform programmes as they were applied to United Nations prisoners of war in Korea and to Chinese intellectuals and Western civilians living in China. I am focusing on these Chinese attempts at persuasion and coercion for several reasons.

One, because of the historical importance of these events;
Two, because the techniques employed by the Chinese are of very great interest to psychologists and have stimulated considerable research in the USA, Britain and elsewhere;
Three, because we can find parallels with various techniques used by past and present religious groups.

Thought reform started in the early days of the Chinese communist movement (the late 1920s) when a scheme of education and propaganda was founded designed to modify 'the whole human being by giving him a totally new view of the world and awakening in him a range of feelings, reactions, thoughts, and attitudes entirely different from those to which he was accustomed' (Ellul, 1965, p. 304). Such education was directed towards the civilian population in areas under communist control and to captured soldiers. The techniques, described in the following sections, were evolved over a period of time. In so far as they were applied by the

Chinese to their own nationals they were designed to integrate individuals into a new political order as firmly as possible and to detach them from their former groups by weakening their traditionally strong family ties and by removing them from their village organizations.

Since the establishment of a Communist government in the whole of mainland China in 1949, a curious blend of continuous education and reform, together with purges of dissidents, has been developed. Ellul (1965) suggests that there have been three aspects of Chinese education and propaganda:

One, the total integration of child education with propaganda;
Two, the development of the discussion system. The aim of such discussion is not to arrive at some ultimate truth or to develop new ideas and understanding but to gain acceptance for a predetermined view;
Three, the notion that there is the need to press people again and again into the mould of the perfect socialist and to ensure absolute conformity by the individual to Maxist doctrine and the new systems of their society.

There are those — such as Marxist sociologists — who would say that the first point above is true of most education systems but not necessarily formally acknowledged. In other words, there may be a 'hidden curriculum'; for instance, when children learn to calculate profits or interest they do not merely acquire mathematical skills but implicitly may also absorb the 'ideology' of capitalism. The second point is superficially reminiscent of Lewin's aims but the emphasis in his groups was for members to arrive *rationally* at new understandings as a basis for action.

Attempts at political indoctrination: prisoners of war of the Chinese during the Korean war

Chronologically, the experiences of the United Nations prisoners of war of the Chinese in the early 1950s came later than the indoctrination or reduction of Chinese intellectuals described in the next section. I am, however, starting our discussion with the experiences of these soldiers for two reasons.

One, Western government and army authorities were unprepared for and shocked by the Chinese attempt at the mass indoctrination of prisoners of war. This was an unexpected and new method of warfare. The Chinese were not merely containing men, as is usual with prisoners of war so that they cannot continue to fight on their own side, but they tried to convert these prisoners to their own view of the world.

Two, previously, American psychologists had studied how best to put across 'persuasive communications' in the context of the values of their own society which they shared. For example, in exploring how health or safety campaigns should be presented to gain adherents or how to get socially useful innovation adopted, they worked within the value system of their society. Now they were faced with an attack from outside their own society on the values generally held in their country. As a consequence, their investigation of the indoctrination programme of the Chinese during the Korean war began to refocus their interest from studying how to put across information and gain acceptance for it to how to help people to *resist* being influenced. Psychologists also began to be more aware of the ethics of using such knowledge as they had in attempting to influence people, whether within their own society or beyond it.

The conditions and experiences of the prisoners of war in Korea are of particular interest to *social* psychologists since such success as the Chinese had depended on their ability to undermine the prisoners' normal social relationships in the camps and with their families through the withholding of mail and news. These prisoners of war were surprised that they were expected to think of themselves as students of politics under the tutelage of their communist guards. They soon learned that their treatment as prisoners of war depended on how far their political convictions pleased their captors. 'Reactionaries' were severely punished.

At the time it was considered disturbing, surprising and incomprehensible that a considerable percentage of American prisoners of war collaborated with the enemy (Schein, 1957; Kinkead, 1959). The extent of collaboration varied from writing anti-American propaganda and information on comrades to less serious offences such as broadcasting Christmas greetings to families at home (and hence putting the Chinese, by implication, in a favourable light). In addition, twenty-one Americans (out of some 4,000 survivors) elected not to return to the United States at the end of the war (though most did so eventually). Only one British soldier out of nearly 1,000 prisoners did not return home. How did the Chinese set about achieving their aims?

First of all, from a psychological point of view, the American, British and other soldiers were ill-prepared and not clearly aware of what they were fighting for. Their Chinese captors surprised them by being, initially, friendly and lenient and willing to treat the prisoners as 'students' to whom they could teach the 'truth' about the war. They explained that the United Nations had entered the war illegally and that prisoners could be shot as war criminals unless they learned what the Chinese wished them to learn, 'namely: that the Communists had a monopoly of truth; that the prisoners accepted that they had been dupes of their capitalist rulers; that they were willing to learn the "truth"; and that they welcomed their "liberation" by the Chinese' (Ministry of Defence, 1955).

Our discussion of total institutions has shown us that people have great difficulty in maintaining their views, their integrity as individuals or their normal behaviour if their social environment is designed to strip them of customary supports and reinforcement to their 'normal selves. The

Chinese, too, aimed at the total control of the prisoners' environment and social milieu. They systematically destroyed the prisoners' formal and informal *group structure*. They put their own men in charge of platoons and companies. They undermined accepted loyalties and discipline by prohibiting distinctions of rank, punishing any officer or NCO who attempted to give an order and encouraged the humiliation of officers. Eventually officers and NCOs were removed to separate camps as 'reactionaries'. The Chinese also tried to undermine informal groupings and relationships by setting men against each other. For example, if during compulsory indoctrination[1] classes (often lasting as long as eight hours at a stretch) a prisoner was recalcitrant the whole group would be made to stand until the prisoner withdrew his remarks or question. After hours of standing the prisoner's comrades would urge him to abandon his objections and he usuallly gave in under moral pressure from his own side. He was made to apologize and his comrades were made to criticize him. From criticism to 'informing' is a relatively small step and the Chinese managed to establish a system of informers so that the men felt they could trust no one. Interrogation often lasting for days was another technique for manipulating the prisoners — a technique only partly intended to elicit useful information. Its main purpose was to undermine the prisoner's trust in each other by the pretence that information had already been obtained from others in the camp. Thus, a person who resisted answering question, despite great fatigue and the continued repetition of the same question, would see that he had resisted in vain when the interrogator pulled out a notebook and read the answer to him, an answer he had obtained elsewhere or had invented. The process would be repeated with a new question till eventually that man felt it was useless to resist further and to suffer in vain. Interrogation was also designed to undermine a person's self-respect since a prisoner of war is not supposed to reveal anything other than his name, rank and number. Once he had given some information, even information he knew the Chinese had already, they could increase their pressures on him to collaborate further by threatening to expose him to his comrades.

Indoctrination sessions during which intensive pressures were brought to bear on single individuals were increasingly practised by the Chinese as the war continued. They proved to be more effective than mass lectures, involving as they did a personal relationship between prisoner and instructor. Not only does a man have to listen (rather than doodle or doze as he might do at a mass meeting) when the argument is directed at him personally, but, as is often the case, his own ability to argue back is limited and he is, therefore, more vulnerable to influence even if, initially, he thinks the argument faulty or specious. In *group indoctrination* classes if no one is swayed, resistance is easier and the Chinese could be made to look foolish when they did not understand slang and idiom sufficiently to appreciate when they were being subtly ridiculed.

The obstruction of communication with home was another means of manipulating and influencing the prisoners. Usually only mail which carried bad news was delivered. The withholding of other letters increased feelings of isolation and insecurity. Parcels, books and magazines were not delivered. Only communist newspapers were available. Men were urged to communicate with relations and friends by making broadcasts which were to include peace 'propaganda'. The Chinese also appreciated that the natural longing of their captives for peace (and hence repatriation) could be channelled into forming 'peace committees' and into making apparently spontaneous appeals which might have a greater impact in the free world than overtly Chinese-orginated 'propaganda'.

It must not be forgotten that psychological pressures or inducements to 'progressive' prisoners of war were backed by 'physical coercion and torture, revolting to the humane mind' Ministry of Defence, 1955). This report gives full details of tortures reported by repatriated British prisoners of war and, independently, American soldiers reported similar tortures (Schein, 1956). Thus, in addition to beatings and imprisonment in tiny cages which were too small to sit, stand or lie in, prisoners were made to stand semi-naked and barefoot on the frozen Yalu river where water which froze immediately was poured over their feet; prisoners were left for hours with their feet frozen into the ice to reflect on their 'crimes'. Another form of torture was to fix a hangman's noose round a prisoner's neck; he was then hoisted up on his toes and the rope fixed so that if he slipped or bent his knees he would hang himself.

To what extent were these pressures and manipulations effective in producing acts of collaboration (broadcasting for the enemy, admitting to participating in germ warfare, informing on other prisoners, and so on) or in producing changes in attitudes or beliefs?

Firstly, collaboration. It would appear that between ten and fifteen per cent of the American prisoners consistently collaborated in a variety of ways with the purposes of their captors and by doing so they, of course, offended against the norms of their own society. This group included people who collaborated for opportunist reasons, such as extra food or privileges, and others who were particularly vulnerable because of their low status in their home community — they often felt they had not had a proper chance in life or else looked on themselves as failures. Still others were simply weak individuals who had initially been tricked into collaboration.

A similar percentage (ten to fifteen per cent) of prisoners did not collaborate at all. They were either those who rebelled consistently against authority — when in the army or when in the situation of prisoners. Others were mature, well-integrated people with a strong sense of personal honour who could withstand the disruption of their normal social organization and support. Others, possibly, denied their strong desire to collaborate by 'reaction formation', that is, the unconscious suppression of this desire in favour of the opposite, strong resistance.

The vast majority of the prisoners, however, 'played it cool', engaging in a certain degree of overt compliance and making minor concessions such as feigning an interest in the indoctrination programme but primarily remaining passive and withdrawn. It would appear from the official British investigation (Ministry of Defence, 1955) that a somewhat smaller percentage of British prisoners collaborated with their Chinese captors. Remarkable also is the record of the Turkish prisoners. A shocking thirty-eight per cent of American prisoners had died during captivity; whilst the living conditions were very inadequate, survival also depends on psychological factors — on 'morale'. None of the Turkish prisoners succumbed because sick and wounded prisoners were supported by their comrades. No Turkish prisoners collaborated. This has been attributed (Kinkead, 1959) to the authoritarian attitudes of the Turks which led to their recognizing only their own superiors as valid sources of information and authority though it has also been suggested that the Chinese lacked Turkish speaking personnel and that that is why they were unable to influence the Turkish soldiers. The American army authorities were greatly disturbed by the lack of morale among those of their soldiers who were taken prisoner and they subsequently developed a new code of behaviour for American soldiers in order to increase their ability to stand their ground mentally and morally as well as physically.

Secondly, what about beliefs? Were many prisoners converted to communism? We have already mentioned that only very few prisoners refused repatriation and some of these may not have been converts to communism but were afraid of facing charges on their return home. Of those who returned one cannot know how many became newly sympathetic to communist views or towards the aims of China in restructuring its society; how many became strengthened in tentative views they may have held prior to their imprisonment; or in how many a more critical attitude to their own society was created. Indeed one may ask which of these outcomes were intended by the Chinese. The important question of how likely it is that prisoners, once returned to their own society, will maintain any new found beliefs will be discussed later (pages 78—85). One point, however, can be raised here. The extent to which the Chinese succeeded in making prisoners collaborate with them was, initially, received with a great deal of shock and surprise, largely because the military, the ordinary public and, to some extent, psychologists too, think of the person as a recognizable individual, wholly him- or herself and behaving in a fairly consistent manner. The fact that collaboration with the enemy (which, in the above view, might be considered inconsistent with what a soldier would do 'normally') took place on an unexpected scale was then explained by Schein (1956, 1957) and others as being due, in part, to the special vulnerability or susceptibilities of some individuals; in larger measure, however, the effects were seen as being due to the control of the total 'milieu' by the Chinese which involved the prisoners in quite unexpected and not previously experienced pressures and harassment. None of us should be so lacking in humility as to predict how we would ourselves be able to stand up to such pressures or, for that matter, how we would respond to the more transient pressures of a religious revivalist meeting. Thus, for instance, many people made a 'decision for Christ' when at a Billy Graham meeting in England in the 1960s, probably without a long-lasting change in beliefs or behaviour. And, as we have seen, in the experiments conducted by Milgram (1974), a high proportion of the subjects could not withstand the short-term psychological pressures created by the experimenter urging them to follow his instructions (though fewer succumbed to his influence when they were with others who were seen to disobey the experimenter). In consequence, they behaved in ways they would not 'normally' engage in, nor had various groups of experts, such as psychiatrists, expected them to act in such ways.

Similarly, even the adoption of a temporary role for payment as prison guard or prisoner in an experiment (Zimbardo *et al.*, 1973) can lead to extraordinary changes in the role-players' perceptions of others and in their behaviour and attitudes towards them. (This study will be further discussed below, pages 85—88). By contrast, the United Nations prisoners of the Chinese and North Koreans endured their conditions of harrassment, torture and control for several years. In essence, a prisoner had several problems: how to remain alive, how to improve his living conditions, how to maintain a consistent outlook on life under conditions where basic values and beliefs were strongly undermined, and how to maintain friendship ties and concern for others under the conditions of mutual distrust, lack of leadership and of social disorganization which the Chinese had created. Whilst their conditions were more extreme, the pressure and procedures, they experienced are remarkably like those Goffman describes as occurring in mental hospitals where the patient, too, has to accept the description of 'reality' offered by the staff in order to ameliorate his conditions.

Was the Chinese indoctrination campaign effective? Certainly, their techniques and behaviour created conditions in which only collaboration and acceptance of communist ideologies led to resolution of the problems the prisoners faced. As we have seen, the majority of prisoners collaborated in various ways from time to time but it is more difficult to assess the extent to which the Chinese were successful in changing beliefs and values though the indoctrination programmes are likely to have had *some* effects at the time and when back home later on, as indicated above. I will return to these issues after we have discussed how the Chinese attempted to influence their own nationals.

Chinese revolutionary colleges and re-education

In this section I am going to discuss methods of 'thought reform' which have much in common with the psychological manipulations reviewed in the last section but go beyond them in their scope and effects.

These more intensive techniques were intended to re-educate rather than to punish or eliminate those citizens who were defined as holding erroneous political views. They were applied by the Chinese primarily to members of their own society, particularly intellectuals. Our main source of information on these 're-education' programmes is the work of Dr R.J. Lifton who in 1954 and 1955 studied some of the failures of the processes of 'thought reform'. He interviewed in Hong Kong twenty-five Westerners and fifteen Chinese intellectuals who had been through these programmes and who had been expelled from mainland China or who had fled from there. 'Thought reform' as practised by the Chinese is interesting from a psychological point of view because it goes beyond normal processes of influence or persuasion such as social pressure, exhortation or ethical appeals. It is the extraordinary, 'combination of external force or coercion with an appeal to inner enthusiasm through evangelistic exhortation which gave thought reform its emotional scope and power' (Lifton, 1961, p. 13).

Lifton (1957) discusses the 'revolutionary colleges' set up all over China in the late 1960s and the techniques developed there for reforming the political views of the population. These colleges were mainly attended by Chinese intellectuals and officials; some were there as the result of thinly veiled threats but most were genuine volunteers eager to equip themselves for an important role in the new communist China. Students usually attended for approximately six months and Lifton distinguishes three stages 'which represent the successive psychological climates to which the student is exposed as he is guided along the path of his symbolic death and rebirth: the Great Togetherness, the Closing in of the Milieu, and Submission and Rebirth' (Lifton, 1957, p. 7). During the first stage the student becomes a member of a ten-person *study group* in which the participants discuss their experiences and their hatred of the old régime. These group experiences are complemented by lectures on the new ideologies and purposes. Then, after four to six weeks, a change begins to develop in the atmosphere — there is a shift in emphasis from the intellectual and ideological to the personal and emotional. Students begin to realize that *they* rather than communist doctrine are the object of study. Their views and attitudes come under scrutiny and the leader and other members of their primary membership group exert pressures on them to adopt the 'correct' views. Constant criticism of others and self-criticism leading to confessions and reform are required of the student. 'Backward'

students with suspicious backgrounds or whose confessions are not keen
enough in criticizing others are singled out, relentlessly criticized,
threatened and publicly humiliated. No student can in these circumstances avoid feelings of fear, anxiety or conflict. All are fearful of being
considered reactionary and found wanting. The last stage of this programme of thought reform is the student's final confession — a document
of 5—25,000 words which is prepared over a period of weeks and which is
read to the group where it is subjected to painful discussion and revision.
When at last this confession is approved the student experiences great
emotional relief. Confession is the symbolic submission to the régime and
at the same time the person's rebirth into the communist community.

Is such thought reform effective? Obviously not in every case; as I have
pointed out, Lifton interviewed students from these revolutionary colleges
who had left China as dissident refugees. Nevertheless, there are many
reasons for assuming that this programme did have wide-ranging effects.
It is, again, the control of the students' environment (what Lifton refers to
as 'milieu control') which makes the programme potentially so awesome
and effective. He writes:

> [the student's] environment is so mobilized that it will psychologically
> support him only if he meets its standards, and will quickly and thoroughly
> undermine him when he fails to do so. More and more there is a blending of
> external and internal milieux, as his own attitudes and beliefs become
> identical with those of his outer environment. (Lifton 1957, p. 13).

In addition, the student experiences the 'emotional catharsis of personal
confession, the relief of saying the unsaid, of holding nothing back. He
attains the rewards of self-surrender, of giving up his individual struggles,
merging with an all-powerful force, and thereby sharing its strength'
(Lifton 1957, p. 18). 'Thought reform' is effective, in certain circumstances, not because students emerge intellectually convinced of the
validity of new information, ideologies or dogmas but because they need,
psychologically, to be members of their immediate group and wider
society in order to have a meaningful existence. If these needs can only be
met by adopting certain values and beliefs, many people will end up by
making such values and beliefs their own. This, indeed, is the crucial
lesson to be learned here in the context of our analysis of group
phenomena.

Short and long-term effects of thought reform

The methods used by the Chinese during the 1950s towards prisoners of
war, their own citizens and Western civilian prisoners aroused, at the
time, a great deal of anxiety and discussion. Several questions remain pertinent even now.

First, are these methods quite different and more destructive of an individual's self-concept and integrity than other methods designed to influence which had been previously employed?

Secondly, what are the long-term effects of mass or individual indoctrination programmes?

With regard to the first question, one can certainly say that the methods employed by the Chinese are not entirely new and their effects not mysterious. Similar psychological techniques had been used by the Russians in their 1930s show trials when Western observers were surprised to see political dissidents admit their crimes of dissent even though they did not look as if they had been beaten up or tortured. They had become convinced of their own guilt since dissent from the party line to a communist *is* a crime. But history is full of people confessing to crimes such as witchcraft which they probably did not commit and, indeed, people make statements at police stations which they later retract. It is relatively easy to disorientate a person by lack of food and sleep, lack of companionship or ignorance of the passage of time (by being kept in a permanently lit or a permanently dark room). Such disorientation makes people suggestible as well as psychologically dependent on an interrogator — their only human contact. The Chinese elaborated on such methods, particularly by their use of relentless group pressure. But is such pressure different in kind or only in degree from the influences exerted by the group over the individual as discussed in Section I? The difference between 'normal' group processes and the manipulations described here probably rests on the lack of other contacts and information over a long period of time which eliminates choice for the individual, reality-testing or consensual validation except when he or she speaks from the 'correct' standpoint. As our brief discussion of Goffman's analysis of total institutions has shown, whether inmates are there voluntarily or not is not the crucial factor which determines the extent to which they are likely to be influenced in their new surroundings. As we have seen, it is the 'stripping' processes people undergo and the lack of choice in human contacts which force a new personality or, in our present context, new political views on him or her. In the mass indoctrination programme of their prisoners of war the Chinese had to attempt to undermine previous social relationships before they could hope to make an impact. The students at their revolutionary colleges, too, were placed into a social context which made it difficult to retain former views. Such relentless pressure from the social milieu, the experience of guilt and release by confession are so effective one wonders whether the torture and hardship inflicted on the prisoners of war were really necessary to achieve 're-education', though no doubt they ensured that people were trapped into acts of collaboration or into making confessions, even phony ones, which then could be used against them.

Although most of my examples have been taken from twentieth-century China, I do not wish you to think that these techniques of persuasion are peculiarly Chinese. Such techniques have been employed by religious bodies and mass movements throughout history. Thus, the Inquisition used coercion; confession, criticism and self-criticism are part of the Catholic religion, of Protestant revivalist groups and of Moral Rearmament. But it is the total control of the social milieu which is the source of the helplessness of the victim.

The methods employed by the Chinese, then, are not wholly new nor specifically Chinese. Nor are they incomprehensible in psychological terms, though they may not have previously been employed so relentlessly or on so many people. Even so, as we have seen, many people do manage to resist doing what is required of them or resist adopting new beliefs. Indeed, one may say that people resist, adapt and conform according to their own deep-seated personalities and many individuals are remakable for the inner resources they can call forth under extreme stress. We have already mentioned that Goffman, somewhat unexpectedly in view of his notion that personality is only a transient stance a person adopts in response to situational expectations, showed that mental patients adapt to their hospital environment in personal and idiosyncratic ways. I have mentioned that among the prisoners of war those who previously were obstreperous towards those in authority continued to resist pressures from the Chinese. Lifton (1961) in his interviews with Western civilians expelled from China also shows that each person responded to his ordeal in terms of his own personality and fundamental beliefs.

Whilst one can describe the techniques used by the Chinese in terms of Western psychological, psychiatric or theological concepts perhaps one still has to ask *why* thought reform was so relentlessly pursued by them. Thought reform certainly is a means of *social control* but the emphasis in the Chinese programme has been on the *reform and redemption of the individual*, not just on repression or purges of dissidents. Their insistence on implementing these processes of thought reform might nevertheless appear destructive of human integrity, identity and dignity to an observer from another cultural tradition. There remain then very important ethical questions.

Interestingly, whilst the 'cultural revolution' has come to an end in China, it would appear that some of these methods are still in use. For instance, a series of television programmes first shown in 1984 on Channel 4 under the title 'The Heart of the Dragon' portrayed the use of group pressure in gaining acceptance for the country's stringent birth control policies. Another of the programmes illustrated the use of group pressure to 'redeem' a confessed thief. The programme showed how she repeatedly had to confess to her crime and, to European eyes, humble herself and acknowledge her deviation from her society's standards. She was sentenced to a year's 'surveillance' which, it was stated, would involve repeated confessions at her place of work and elsewhere. Control through group membership, coupled with the 're-education' of the individual, therefore, still seem important processes through which to achieve conformity and social cohesion in present-day China.

How can we answer our second question concerning the long-term effects of the methods used by the Chinese?

We have seen in discussing Kelman's model (page 24) that the psychological effects of group membership may persist even when the individual is no longer a member of the group. Such effects on values or behaviour persist if individuals have made the group's standards their own and, therefore, do not need the support of the group to maintain their new-found beliefs. However, people tend to adopt new views or new ways of behaving as their own only if they fit in with other important values they already hold or if they offer a way of attaining goals they have previously accepted or set for themselves.

Political indoctrination of Western prisoners of war, as we have seen, was relatively ineffective even in the short run. Acts of collaboration do not necessarily imply acceptance of new political doctrines; they may merely indicate a strategy for survival. Once a soldier returns home, even if he has adopted new views, he is unlikely to maintain his views in a society which does not support them. Some who have made the new views their own, of course, did not return home but stayed in China. Even then some returned later. Nevertheless, if we can draw a parallel to the follow-up study of the women who had been at Bennington College (discussed on page 10) we may speculate that those who had adopted new views during their captivity might on their return have sought out like-minded people and information to support their new beliefs.

The Chinese students emerging from the Chinese revolutionary colleges were in a different psychological situation. They returned to a society which upheld and supported the ideas and values they had adopted in the colleges.

In assessing the likelihood of people changing their values when subjected to intense, orchestrated pressure one must consider three interlocking aspects:

(a) a person's initial values, attitudes, knowledge, on the one hand, and his or her personal susceptibility to succumb to pressures, on the other;
(b) the techniques employed by the change-agent, the extremity of the situation in which the person finds him- or herself and the length of time during which a person is isolated from contrary, outside influences;
(c) the social situation into which the individual emerges — whether or not it is supportive of new views or behaviour he or she may have adopted.

The above three criteria apply to most situations in which change is expected of a person. Thus, less drastically, successful socialization into a professional role, or learning to be an accepted member of a school community, or equipping oneself to be an officer of one's country's armed forces all depend on the interplay of these three factors. Therefore, what I have termed 'coercion' is only an extreme version of influence processes occurring constantly around us. What makes 'coercion' different is the *extremity* of the measures employed, particularly the isolation of the individual from his or her previous group membership.

The desired political effects of coercive methods can be shown to be limited and dependent on antecedent personal characteristics as well as on post-treatment situational factors. Nevertheless, Lifton's case studies (Lifton, 1961) would suggest that people are unlikely to emerge unchanged from the insights they have gained through these intensive onslaughts on their thoughts and the self-questioning which it provoked. They may be stronger, having undergone extreme physical and psychological pain and come out of their experiences with some degree of self-respect. At times, however, the insights gained into repressed and previously unknowable aspects of the mind may well have left them shaken and disturbed. Indeed, to a minor extent, the same could be said of Milgram's subjects who needed careful 'debriefing' to adjust to their disturbing experiences.

In my analysis of mass-indoctrination and re-education I have endeavoured to account for these phenomena in terms of the relationship of the individual to his or her immediate groups and to the wider social context. But are there other psychological theories which can help us understand the processes at work?

I have previously mentioned the theory of cognitive dissonance proposed by Festinger (1957). This theory suggests that where a person has attitudes, feelings or beliefs which are incompatible or dissonant, the person will feel uncomfortable and be motivated to reduce the dissonance. This can be done by changing some of these cognitions by 'forgetting' or repressing non-fitting views or by re-evaluating some views or preferences and by seeking to strengthen others by obtaining additional information or social support and by avoiding further dissonant information. Thus a heavy smoker may neglect to read articles which link smoking and lung cancer. However, where the dissonance is between a person's behaviour and his or her cognitions, then it is the latter which, according to Festinger, will need to change since the behaviour, once engaged in, cannot be undone. Thus one might expect that a prisoner of war, once he has engaged in an act of collaboration, would change his attitudes, feelings and beliefs about his Chinese captors. However, this is not, as we have seen, what on the whole has happened. But a development derived from dissonance theory may throw a light on the prisoners' situation. Festinger and Carlsmith (1959) demonstrated in a series of experiments, that where a subject in an experiment feels *forced* to engage in behaviour which is incompatible with the subject's beliefs, then *no* change of beliefs occurs. It is suggested that in these *forced compliance* situations the subject does not experience dissonance as he or she feels that compliance was *justified* because of external pressures. Since no dissonance occurs, no change in belief occurs either. These experiments suggest that less attitude change would take place in the kind of conditions to which the prisoners of war were exposed than if less pressure had been applied to them.

Whilst it is quite gratifying to see that the *forced compliance* paradigm which evolved out of laboratory experiments does not contradict the findings concerning these prisoners of war, one is nevertheless on dangerous ground if one relies on an explanation based on temporary and uninvolving laboratory situations to account for these much more pervasive, long-lasting and harrowing events.

Much more potentially interesting ideas to account for attitude change (where it occurs) can be derived from Freud. He described the process of taking someone else's values as one's own as *identification* (the process Kelman would describe as *internalization*). In its original formulation identification was seen to achieve the resolution of the child's Oedipus complex through identification with the father, a feared competitor for the mother's affection. This view was elaborated by later psychoanalysts as accounting for 'identification with the aggressor'. Thus Bettelheim (1943) observed when himself a prisoner at the Dachau Concentration Camp how some prisoners in German concentration camps identified with their captors, decked themselves out in bits of Nazi uniforms and adopted the views of their guards. The deprivations they had undergone had reduced them to a childlike state of dependence on their all-powerful captors. More recently it has been found that victims of hijacks or hostages in holdups also form relationships with their captors, come to like them or to agree with them, even though, or precisely perhaps because, they are dependent on them (Jenkins, 1975), as are the naive subjects dependent on experimenters or their collaborators in conformity and obedience experiments. (See figure 9 for an example of this phenomenon). Patti Hearst is perhaps the most extreme and best known example of this psychological dependence on captors which led to her adopting the role and identity of 'Tania' and apparently joining in the pursuits of the 'Symbionese Liberation Army'.

In her own book (Hearst, 1983) she gives an account of her extraordinary experiences during her captivity. Incidentally, Dr Lifton whom I mentioned for his research on returning soldiers and on dissidents and refugees from China, was one of the expert defence witnesses at her trial, the implication being that her experiences paralleled those of the prisoners of war and those subjected to thought reform in Chinese revolutionary colleges.

You may recall that when the American hostages in Teheran were released in 1980 after more than a year's captivity, they were not, as one

Can those siege friendships last?

Some hostages released from the American Embassy in Teheran last week expressed a vague sympathy towards their Iranian captors. Their attitude must have been partly influenced by concern for those still held but psychiatrists acknowledge that a friendly relationship often develops between captors and captives. Can such a forced friendship survive? JOHN SHIRLEY reports:

WHEN an Italian restaurant manager named Giovanni Scrano emerged unshaven from his ordeal at the Spaghetti House Siege in October, 1975, he astonished almost everyone by speaking out in favour of the leader of the robbers who had held him at gun-point for six days and nights in a windowless basement room.

Scrano visited his former captor, Franklin Davies, in Brixton prison, taking gifts of fruit, cigarettes and cake; he organised a collection among his fellow hostages to buy Davies a Christmas present; and he offered to give *defence* evidence when Davies and his co-conspirators went on trial.

It was an eloquent testimony to the theory of " transference " which predicts that, if left long enough in a calm, secure environment, captors and captives will gradually relate to one another. During sieges police rely on this, believing that it increases their chances of persuading the captors to release their hostages unharmed.

The tactics have often worked and official interest in the unusual " friendships " naturally fades. So, no doubt, do most of the friendships. But last week The Sunday Times discovered that in the case of the " Spaghetti House friendship," the relationship is extraordinarily strong four years after the event.

Scrano visited Davies, on remand in jail, twice a week for nine months. After Davies was sentenced to 21 years for armed robbery and assault, the Home Office stopped the visits because Davies, as a top-security prisoner, could not see anyone he had not known before the robbery.

So they exchanged letters. Scrano arranged a bank account for Davies and paid in small regular amounts so Davies could buy cigarettes, stamps and small luxury items in jail. He sent him books at his request—on politics, revolution and black studies. When Davies wanted to learn a language, Scrano posted him two French and German dictionaries.

In March this year Scrano went abroad. I tracked him down last week to the Pinnochio Restaurant in Monte Carlo, where he is a manager—and where he was finishing his latest weekly letter to Davies.

" We write about the daily hardships of our lives," he said. " Running a restaurant is not always easy, and being in prison is a difficult life. I tell him news about my family and he gives me advice. He says I should be careful, and be sure to be honest in my dealings with other people.

" I think he is a wonderful man. We have formed a creative and close friendship. I am his only contact with the outside world."

During the siege, says Scrano, " We realised we had much in common. We were both foreigners working in a hostile land. I am from southern Italy. In my country, that is like being a black man in England." Davies was the leader who persuaded the others to give up, says Scrano. " I hope we shall remain in contact until he is free again."

FIGURE 9. Affinity between hostage and captor

SOURCE: Sunday Times, November, 25th, 1979.

might expect, immediately flown home to be reunited with their families but were sent to an American base in Wiesbaden, West Germany, as the American authorities feared that they would be too disorientated to cope with family relationships and that it would be necessary to provide professional help for their 're-entry' problems into normal society. In the light of what we know about captor/captives relationships we must assume that the Americans feared that their fellow citizens had been affected in their views by their dependence on their captors.

Further research

As I have explained, the psychological pressures and indoctrination programmes employed against Allied prisoners of war, whilst not unique in kind (though perhaps in scale), aroused great anxiety in the West and raised questions about the nature of loyalty and treason and the preparation of soldiers for captivity. For this reason, the returning prisoners of war were extensively studied by the military, psychologists and psychiatrists in several countries, and much research was subsequently undertaken, often financed by military authorities. For instance, Hebb (Hebb *et al.* (1952) quoted by Watson (1980)) studied the disorientating effects of sensory and sleep deprivation for the Defence Research Board in Canada; and Zimbardo (1973), supported by the US Office of Naval Research, set up a fake prison to study the interpersonal dynamics of imprisonment. From such research lessons have been learnt on how to resist indoctrination and the stresses of captivity. Some of these lessons have been incorporated into military training. Perhaps you will find the implications of Zimbardo's study (outlined in Box 10) as disturbing as the indoctrination programmes I have described.

Box 10   Zimbardo's prison study (Zimbardo et al. 1973).

Zimbardo recruited volunteers (whose normality was checked across a number of psychiatric dimensions) to participate in a study of prison life. The volunteers were allocated at random to the roles of prisoners or guards — the random allocation is, of course, crucial or else it might have been thought that the more dominant or aggressive people had volunteered to be guards. The experiment was intended to last for two weeks but had to be stopped after five days as the guards became more and more aggressive and exhibited a remarkable ability to torment, exploit and dehumanize the inmates. By contrast, the prisoners became apathetic, disturbed and childish and developed psychosomatic symptoms.

These results, like Milgram's findings, demonstrate how easily people can come to behave in 'uncharacteristic' ways when placed into new physical and social situations and are given the chance to adopt new roles, even temporarily. Both studies testify to 'the power of social, institutional forces to make good men engage in evil deeds' (Zimbardo, 1973). One finding, which is of importance in our present context, was that the prisoners did not manage to form a cohesive and supportive group, in fact they deprecated each other. The implication is that, had they managed to form such groups, they could have maintained their normal identity more successfully. A lesson to be learned, then, for life in captivity, is to form bonds with others and, rather than focus on the conditions of imprison-ment, prisoners should use every opportunity to escape mentally from it. Much earlier Bettelheim (1943) who managed to survive a Nazi con-centration camp found that by studying his fellow prisoners he had a purpose in life and this prevented him from succumbing to despair.

Whilst the lessons to be learnt from such post-Korean research undoubtedly can be used to prepare people to withstand pressures in the event they are taken prisoners the very same research, of course, also pin-points how to carry out effective interrogations, how to disorientate prisoners and weaken their resistance and such methods, unfortunately, seem to be in use in many countries.

Zimbardo's study, whilst stemming from post-Korean concerns, is of course also of importance in relation to the administration of prisons (or of other 'total institutions') and the training of the staff of such organi-zations. His findings parallel Goffman's views, reported earlier, that it is the creation and maintenance of social distance between staff and inmates which are the basis of the coercive power of the staff.

Zimbardo has been criticized, as was Milgram, for setting up expe-riments in which subjects are 'deceived, humiliated or maltreated' (Savin, 1973). Others have questioned the way in which Zimbardo and his colleagues have interpreted their findings. Thus Banuazizi and Movahedi (1975) point out that the behaviour of the guards and prisoners may have arisen from the stereotypic expectations of how prisoners and guards behave which they held *prior* to becoming subjects in this experiment. Their behaviour, therefore, cannot be wholly attributed to their reactions to their own experiences in the roles to which they were allocated. The authors argue that the subjects brought 'mental sets' or 'dispositions' or 'culturally conditioned images' to the situation and that these influenced how they behaved in response to the simulated prison environment. In fact, the authors question whether role-playing ever corresponds to a 'real' experience and whether the use of role playing is a suitable methodology for 'testing dispositional versus situational hypotheses' which they take to be a primary goal of the study by Zimbardo and his colleagues. The points they raise are interesting but their view concerning the streotypical expectations subjects have about these roles are possibly more applicable

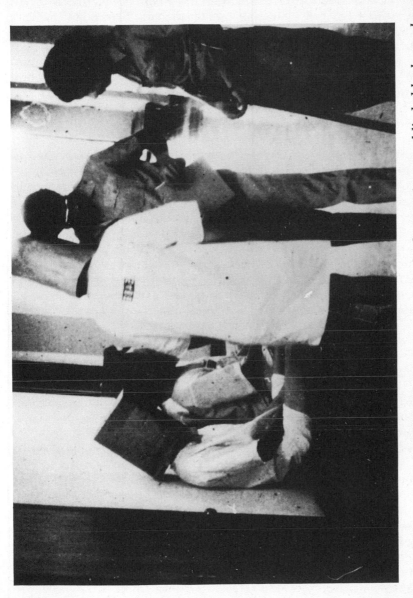

FIGURE 10. This photograph from Zimbardo's prison study shows prisoners, blinded by bags placed over their heads, awaiting a parole board hearing and guards in military style uniforms.
SOURCE: Zimbardo et al. (1973) Copyright Philip Zimbardo

to the role of guard than to that of prisoner. Very few people, if asked to describe how prisoners feel and behave, would have anticipated the extreme reactions of the prisoners in this study. We may also wonder whether these authors would attribute the behaviour of Milgram's subjects to the stereotypic views they had of teachers. How many teachers have they encountered who give electric shocks to pupils who make mistakes? Bettelheim, whom I mentioned earlier, made a point which may be applicable to Zimbardo's student prisoners. He described (Bettelheim, 1943) how respectble, law-abiding middle-class people, thrown into a concentration camp, could not cope with being viewed as criminals and quickly succumbed to the pressures of imprisonment. In the same way, these students may have experienced greater stress than hardened criminals would in the same context.

There is, of course, also another factor which may have contributed to how these students behaved in their respective roles. It has been demonstrated (Orne, 1962) that subjects like to be 'good' subjects and behave in accordance with the perceived expectations of the experimenter and these were perhaps only too obvious — there was a prison (rigged up in the basement of Stanford University), a warden (Zimbardo) and guards and prisoners. However none of these factors — culturally conditioned expectations and the perceived demand characteristics of the experiment — quite account for the extreme reactions the simulated prison environment provoked in the participants, both guards and prisoners, and the main conclusion, that the situational context is a powerful influence on behaviour and experience, still stands.

Mass suicide and cult membership

The most dramatic real life example of the way in which situational pressures overwhelm people is provided by the mass suicide that occurred in an American cult in the 1970s. On November 18th, 1978, over 900 people committed suicide at Jonestown in Guyana. What took place on that day caused shock and dismay in the United States and elsewhere. My reason for including this tragic and disturbing event in this section is that the accounts which have been published (amongst others: Yee and Layton, 1981; Sorrell, 1978; Naipaul, 1981; Dwyer, 1979) suggest firstly, that the techniques practised by the cult leader, the Reverend Jim Jones, closely correspond to those I have already described as having taken place in Korea and China, and secondly, that one cannot begin to understand these events unless one sees them as part of a larger social scene.

Jim Jones was a self-appointed Messiah who founded the People's Temple which attracted many who wanted to escape the pressures of modern society and find new forms of spiritual experience. At the beginning, his community in San Farcisco was engaged in anti-racist and humanitarian work; it was multiracial and Jones saw himself as fighting civil and religious corruption. He became paranoid about the (possibly imaginary) dangers posed to his movement by the CIA, and FBI and others and eventually transferred his community (having failed to be allowed to settle in Russia) to the jungles of Guyana to create an ideal society based on agriculture in the virgin forest. Here, even more than he had managed to do in California, he was able to isolate his followers from outside influences and to control their lives minutely. Individuals were, in addition, subjected to a barrage of propaganda and indoctrination, to forced confessions of 'crimes' and sexual activities and to physical punishments. People were also weakened through hard labour, frequent fasting, poor nutrition, lack of sleep and constant chanting of slogans. Families were broken up and divided (Yee and Lyaton, 1981), other instance of robbing people of customary support. Whilst we may accept that Jones was a charismatic leader,[2] the extent of his control over his followers was based on the techniques he used to influence them as well as their isolation in what can only be described as a concentration camp in the jungle which was policed by armed guards. To bind his followers even more closely to him, as Hitler and others have done, he pointed to hostile groups outside the community and created the delusion that they were threatened by outsiders. As part of his cult, his followers were made to engage in repeated rehearsals of mass suicide on the grounds that suicide was preferable to the fate that might await them if they were attacked by outside forces.

Mass suicides have historical precedents, from Masada in a.d. 73 where 960 Jews chose death rather than become Roman slaves, to the mass suicides of Japanese soldiers and civilians on Saipan to avoid being taken prisoners (a shameful condition for the Japanese of that period[3]) by the Americans towards the end of the Second World War. The threat to Jonestown, however, was largely imaginary, though the actual act of mass suicide was triggered off by the visit (and murder) of US Congressman Ryan who had come at the behest of anxious relatives who had been unable to get in touch with members of their families at Jonestown, and the decision of two families to use his visit to leave the community. Whilst there were no survivors at Jonestown, we have a clear picture of the events of that day as the whole macabre proceedings were tape-recorded and Figure 11 shows some of the dead.

Whilst other contemporary cults in Western society, particularly prevalent in California (see Naipaul, 1981), have not had such tragic outcomes, it is worth noting that the Reverend Jones and his People's Temple were only one of many cults springing up at that time, all fired by the need people may have to believe in some thing beyond their own, perhaps insignificant and banal, existence and a desire for social justice and equality. Membership of cults or sects may satisfy these needs as well as provide relief from internal turmoil. It is possible that these various cults

FIGURE 11.   *Jonestown, Guyana, 21/11/78: bodies lay strewn about a vat containing a cyanide-laced drink.*
SOURCE: *UPI 1949807.*

developed in response to the decline of organized religion and of parental authority and in the search for a meaningful life in a period of great social changes and disillusion. All such cults which have succeeded in establishing themselves have used similar techniques to disengage people from their normal contexts. Thus, for instance, the Moonies start by getting their potential followers to renounce their families and to give up their personal property: both may imply that, should they want to leave, they have nowhere to turn to and no means of escape. The next step is to fasten them to the beliefs which are being advocated by incorporating them into new group memberships, by indoctrination, confessions and public commitment — all methods we have already encountered in discussing thought reform and the indoctrination of prisoners of war.

Whilst such cults engulf only a small minority of people and are, therefore, an unusual milieu, they illustrate the fact that an individual's behaviour and experience need to be understood in terms of his or her group memberships and the groups, in turn, must be viewed as part of the wider social structure and of current ideologies.

Recently the mass media have highlighted attempts by parents or their agents to snatch back their children from the sects they have joined. These young people, having been forcibly removed, are often subjected to 'deprogramming' procedures which may be quite horrific and raise questions of legality and ethics. Ungerleider and Wellisch (1979) report that

> these procedures vary widely and may range from gentle rap sessions to sleep deprivation and sensory overload, with marathon-type encounters that feature shouting, repetitious derogations of the cult, isolation of the person from former associates, moving the deprogrammee from place to place within a period of days, and, occasionally, use of physical force in the event that he or she tries to leave or escape.

How effective such 'deprogramming' is, is likely to depend on the reasons which led a person to join a cult and the extent to which such membership had met the individual's psychological needs. Many young 'deprogrammees' rejoin their cults but at the same time others leave of their own volition without undergoing deprogramming.

Conclusions to Section II

In this section we have ranged very widely — from persuasion, decision making, the relationship between leaders and followers, the experiences of prisoners and hijack victims, to mass suicide and membership of religious cults.

Common to all the research and real life material was the attempt to influer e people through group membership, though the techniques employed ranged from self-persuasion to torture and coercion.

We started with the study of persuasion and showed that the acceptance or rejection of persuasive communications is influenced by the recipients' group membership. Indeed, as you will remember, research on mass media influences arose from the fear that people were helpless *vis-à-vis* media influences but the research led to a revision of this view and to the 'rediscovery of the group' and the importance of interpersonal relations in mediating information from the mass media to the individual.

We then explored the work of Lewin who not only thought that group discussions would lead to the acceptance of new ideas or solutions but that the outcome of group discussions would be the adoption of more *rational* decisions or views. As I have pointed out, for him there was a close relationship between reason and the democratic process.

In discussing leadership we again started with Lewin and his ideas on leadership style affecting the atmosphere of a group, the subjective experience of its members and the group's productivity. Exploring leadership further we saw that it could only be properly understood in the context of the needs of the group members and in the context of the wider society and its norms and ideologies.

We then moved to exploring situations in which people were taken from their normal surroundings and normal group memberships — people in mental hospitals, monasteries, prisoners of war camps, in revolutionary colleges or in virgin forest (as members of a religious sect) and, indeed, in psychological experiments. In all these examples we saw that it is easier to disorientate an individual thus divorced from the normal supports to his or her identity. We also saw that new group memberships could be explicitly used to get the individual to adopt new views. We explored the likelihood of such indoctrination processes leading to relatively permanent changes in an individual's outlook. Implicit in our discussion is the question of how far individuals have a stable and continuing existence outside the groups which provide and support their conception of themselves. Some of the evidence I presented seems to show that there is often a personal core or self which struggles to maintain itself. Other studies, and particularly those concerned with mass suicide, would point to the supremacy of the group over the individual. Primary group membership protects the individual from unwanted and undue outside influences. But, equally, when manipulated in the way described in this section, it is a powerful tool to force new views on the individual whether this process is referred to as 'coercion' or as 're-education'.

SECTION III

Intergroup Relations and Conflicts: From Prejudice to Outgroup Rejection

Our main focus so far has been on the psychological influences at work between individuals who belong to the *same* group (*intragroup relations*) *and the accompanying or consequent cognitive, affective or behavioural changes in the individuals who form the group* (*intraindividual changes*). We have seen that people can be members of, that is, psychologically relate themselves to, many different groups and we have referred to such groups, depending on the context in which we studied them, as primary groups, membership or reference groups. In discussing minority influence I have also used the concept of the outgroup and this concept, together with its counterpart, the ingroup, plays an important role in the study of *intergroup relations*. Those social units of which the member feels psychologically a part can be said to constitute his or her ingroups, those of which people do not feel a part and from which they wish to differentiate themselves constitute their outgroups — and one person's outgroup is, of course, another's ingroup.

The study of intergroup relations focuses on relations between small primary groups (including the temporary groups set up by psychologists in the laboratory) as well as on the relations between groups, such as national or racial groups, which have through history developed their own distinct cultural and social characteristics.

On the primary group level, there is some evidence (which we will explore) that the psychological satisfaction to be gained by group membership is enhanced by the existence of an outgroup, whether real or imaginary. Indeed we shall see that, at any rate in the laboratory, quite arbitrarily defined ingroups will discriminate in the distribution of rewards to equally arbitrarily defined outgroups for apparently the sole purpose of creating and experiencing the satisfaction of ingroup membership.

Outside the laboratory, too, we have ample evidence that people tend to categorize themselves as members of distinct racial or ethnic[4] groups or as members of distinct language, religious or ideological groups (even though they may also be part of a larger grouping such as a nation). Other ingroup/outgroup identifications may distinguish between 'labour' and 'management', the skilled and unskilled, the young and old, men and women, striker and non-striker, the left and the ultra-left or between rival groups of fans at football matches, and so on.

One question we need to face in the exploration of intergroup relations concerns the origins of such self-categorizations. Are they primarily based on the need to feel part of a group? And if there is such a need, is it satisfied by setting oneself and one's group apart from members of other groups? As we shall see, in certain circumstances this process of differentiation is an important psychological mechanism. However, it would be simple-minded in the extreme to attribute the problems of race relations or worker — management relations to purely psychological processes since such relations have a long history which includes economic or legal discrimination which, in turn, has led to inequalities in status and in access to rewards. On a psychological level, identification with an ingroup is often created or strengthened by rejection or discrimination from a dominant outgroup (though whether a person considers the psychological gain of identification with a group sufficient compensation for the discrimination or persecution suffered is another question). Thus, German Jews who thought of themselves as Germans, emancipated from former ghetto communities and assimilated to German culture, were made aware of, and began to focus again on Jewish culture and beliefs in the wake of persecution in the 1930s and the transition from one group identification to another must have been painful for quite a few people. Therefore the question needs to be raised as to whether 'labelling' minority groups as Jews, Blacks, Catholics, the unemployed, the old or whatever other categories might be available, makes people create for themselves an identity distinct from that of other groups when otherwise they might not have done so? The slogan 'black is beautiful' is an indication of a stronger ingroup identification and the development of a new and positive self-image as a response to hostility and discrimination from outside the group. It is quite possible that, in the absence of rejection or discrimination from others, religious or racial minorities would think of themselves as members of the larger group, such as the nation, of which they also form a part. Individuals can thus be propelled into group membership which may, previously, not have been very *salient* to them and it is likely that they will increasingly come to recognize these groups as relevant ingroups for themselves in a variety of contexts. In this country, many Commonwealth immigrants arrived with the idea that they were British, that they would form part of the British community but, quite often, they have retreated from this view and formed a stronger identification with their country of origin because of the social categorizations forced on them by the host community. This is a particularly difficult problem for the children of immigrants who feel rejected, though born in England, and who initially, no longer had a strong affinity or links with the country from which their parents came. But over a period of time, some of the young West Indians in Britain came to identify themselves with movements such as Rastafarianism which symbolized to them their links with their or their parents' countries of origin.

Identification with a group, then, depends not only on the self-perceived differences between one's own group and others but also on the attitudes of members of other groups who may force an unsought for distinction of one's own group from others by 'labelling' or other psychological processes or by the short or long term creation of inequalities between two groups (through exclusion from opportunities or through physical segregation in ghettoes).

The study of intergroup relations has long been a topic of interest to social psychologists. Thus, the study of prejudice and discrimination and of race relations figure in early American social psychology textbooks. The study of immigrant groups, their origins, development and adjustments to American society also proved to be a focus of great interest as is evidenced in the classic five-volume work on *The Polish Peasant in Europe and America* (Thomas and Znaniecki, 1918). Social psychologists have interested themselves in these questions in part because intergroup relations are often fraught with conflict (and social psychologists hope to contribute to the resolution of such conflicts) and in part because intergroup relations are a truly *social* psychological topic as it focuses on those relations between individuals which are determined to a considerable extent, not by their personal relationships or individual characteristics, but by their membership of different social groups. A very good example of this is the conflict between Protestants and Catholics in Northern Ireland, a conflict with a three hundred year tradition of hostility, the present manifestations of which cannot be attributed to hostility between individuals for personal reasons.

We shall now turn to explore the questions and issues which are currently of active concern to social psychologists in their search for an understanding of intergroup relations and conflict. Basically, social psychologists have considered a range of questions (which are not mutually exclusive).

They have explored (and continue to do so)

one, whether intergroup relations or conflicts stem from the attitudes or other predispositions people have towards the outgroup;

two, whether competition or conflict generate negative evaluation of or attitudes to the outgroup and, whether, once such an outlook is established, it may not only be difficult to dislodge but may increase conflict, competition and tension between two groups;

three, whether the mere psychological process of categorizing oneself as a member of one group leads to discrimination against the members of another group.

four, whether prejudice and discrimination have effects on the self-concept and/or the achievements of members of a minority group; and

five in what contexts bystanders will come to the aid of a stranger who needs help.

We will now look at these issues in turn.

Attitudes and prejudice

In Section II we have seen that situational determinants may override and blot out a person's predispositions. Thus we have witnessed the norm-setting influence of the majority in a group, the effects of a consistent behavioural style when adopted by a minority or the overwhelming effects of immersing oneself into the role of prisoner or guard. In spite of such evidence both psychologists and the general public think of people as being reasonably consistent in their attitudes and of acting in accordance with their attitudes, values, beliefs or personalities — hence the dismay and surprise at Zimbardo's or Milgram's findings. People of course do behave in ways which reflect their values and world views since mostly they have chosen to be in situations and occupy roles in which they can act in accordance with their underlying beliefs and attitudes. And their attitudes and beliefs, of course, broadly reflect those prevalent in their society and which they have adopted (and adapted) through growing up in that society. Thus their behaviour 'normally' is likely to reflect their personalities as well as being appropriate to the situation. By contrast, in the last chapter we discussed studies in which the focus was on the impact of unusual and *imposed* contexts. In fact, we saw that when the focus was on changing people, as in Goffman's study of mental hospitals, the inmates were first systematically robbed of the 'props' to their personalities and, we also saw, similar efforts were necessary before indoctrination or thought reform could be attempted. In other studies subjects were placed into ambiguous or novel situations (for instance in Sherif's experiments on the autokinetic effect) so that they could not make use of such knowledge or attitudes as they had and thus these experiments also show the impact of situational aspects (in Sherif's experiment the estimates made by others).

The study of the development and change of attitudes and their relation to a person's behaviour is one of the most important research areas of social psychology. In this book we cannot delve into all these issues and the theories which have been evolved but we need to look at research and theories which have a bearing on understanding intergroup behaviour. The most important topic in this context is the study of the genesis and effects of *prejudice*. Attitudes tend to be seen as having three components. One, a *cognitive component* which reflects what people know and think about an issue. Two, an *affective component* which denotes their *feeling* about an issue. And three, a *behavioural component* which is seen as a predisposition to *behave* in a particular way towards the object of the attitude. It is important to understand that we are referring here to a predisposition to, rather than a prediction of, the actual behaviour, as the link between knowledge and beliefs, feelings and behaviour is not simple or straightforward. Thus we have seen in Section II examples of behaviour which under environmental pressures were divorced from people's 'normal' attitudes or other dispositions. Also, we have seen there that, according to dissonance theory, attitudes may develop or change in the wake of behaviour and hence to state that attitudes predispose towards certain behaviour is not necessarily correct; the relationship may be the other way round. A great deal of attitude research stems from the desire to elucidate the complex and manifold links between attitudes and behaviour, that is, attitudes were not only studied as a subject in its own right but because of the relationship between attitudes and behaviour.

Attitudes are learned in the society in which we grow up and live. Such prejudices as we may hold or act on may be the cultural 'norm' of the society we live in and may reflect the social representations we may hold of certain outgroups or minority groups. However, prejudiced attitudes may also be seen as part of an individual's personality and resulting from a certain cognitive style. In the next section I will discuss a study which focuses on this issue.

The authoritarian personality

Towards the end of the Second World War a group of researchers in California became concerned with exploring the psychological roots of anti-semitism and, more generally, the psychological predispositions which would render an individual *susceptible* to prejudice and to anti-democratic propaganda. Some of the members of this group had emigrated from Nazi Germany where they had experienced the rise of fascism at first hand. Whilst their orientation in commenting on the problems of their society when working in their *Institute for Social Research* in Frankfurt had been primarily based on Marxist economic and philosophic theories they came increasingly to think that such an analysis had to be supplemented by psychological understanding; in particular, they felt the need to explore the unconscious roots of ideology. Not surprisingly therefore they attempted 'to fill the psychological gap in Marx' (Billig, 1982) by using psychoanalytic theories and concepts to understand the relationship between 'collective ideologies' such as fascism and the individual's psychology. Their study became a classic in social psychology (though it also generated much criticism). The authors came to call their book and the personality type they identified *The authoritarian personality*. This study is described in Box 11.

Box 11   The authoritarian personality (Adorno, Levinson, Frenkel-Brunswick and Sanford, 1950).

The basic theoretical proposition in *The authoritarian personality* is the psychoanalytic concept of displacement. This suggests that children whose parents severely limit their expression of sexual and aggressive urges will grow into adults who need to redirect those repressed urges onto external objects, such as minority groups. Prejudice in this formulation is seen as arising from a developmental sequence and the externalization or expression of ego-defensive processes and a person's political views as reflecting deep-seated aspects of the personality. The researchers had found support for this proposition in a number of ways. Their sample of 2000 subjects consisted of college students and other native born, white, non-Jewish middle class people. They were interviewed about their political views and their childhood experiences; projective tests were used to encourage people to express their unconscious or normally concealed attitudes to minority groups; the authors also developed and administered several attitude scales measuring beliefs about antisemitism, ethnocentrism and political/economic conservatism. Later the so-called F- (for fascism) scale, which is still used, was developed to measure anti-democratic tendencies in the personality without reference to specific ideological beliefs. On the basis of these measures the researchers built psychological profiles of the twenty-five per cent of the most prejudiced and, by contrast, of the twenty-five per cent of the least prejudiced subjects in their sample. The authoritarian person came to be seen as having a syndrome of attributes which were linked and a set of interconnected attitudes which comprised his or her world view. Such a person is described as rigid, dogmatic, servile to authority, contemptuous of weakness, lacking in cognitive complexity, low in tolerance for ambiguity and high in prejudice.

I have previously pointed out that the experimental method (as used by Asch, Milgram and Zimbardo) favours the making of *situational* explanations. By contrast, the psychometric measures (interviews, projective tests, attitude scales, and so on) employed by the authors of *The authoritarian personality* and the use by these researchers of psycho-analytic concepts of personality development builds in a bias favouring *dispositional* attributions, that is, the explanation for what happened in Germany is in terms of the emergence of a particular personality type. More generally one might say that this focus on the individual's moti-vation or pathology directs attention away from the deficiencies of the wider social system.

The research on the authoritarian personality has impinged on popular consciousness and it has also stimulated methodological and theoretical critiques. One such criticism that the original research on the autho-ritarian personality was based on 'the preconceived idea that authorita-rianism is a characteristic of the right and the corresponding notion that there is no authoritarianism on the left' (Shils 1954, p. 32), has led to attempts to develop a measure of authoritarianism equally applicable to the left and right. Thus Rokeach (1960) attempted to find a politically unbiased measure of authoritarianism (or, as he called it, *dogmatism*). His dogmatism scale attempted to pinpoint open/closed mindedness but he found it difficult to find closed mindedness in people who held left-wing political views. Perhaps this is due to the fact that at the time when he carried out his studies in the United States in the 1950s to be left-wing was against the majority trend. Left-wing people, therefore, initially, at any rate, had to think out their views and had come to distance themselves from the majority. This would imply open-mindedness and cognitive complexity. Eysenck (1954), working in England, distinguished between a dimension of political belief (right and left wing) and a dimension of tender/tough mindedness, the latter corresponding to authoritarianism and in his view 'tough mindedness' can be associated with left wing beliefs and a tough-minded person will be attracted to an extreme political ideology, be that fascism on the right or communism on the left. Both Rokeach and Eysenck have been criticized; in particular it has been alleged that the scales they developed to test their theories were not well balanced between left wing and right wing statements and therefore lacked validity (Billig, 1979). Whether or not these criticisms are justified, totalitarian movements on the right as well as on the left tend to demand uncritical adherence to the party line from their followers; it is likely that such movements would attract people who are predisposed to conform to such demands. However, this point, too, is not straightforward or simple. *Joining* a party may be psychologically different from *staying* with it. People may join a party as a reaction to particular issues, policies or injust-ices in their society; later such members may leave if they cannot associate themselves with the full ideology of a party or its demands for the acceptance of party doctrine. We should also recognize that the act of joining the communist party in Britain, where it is a minority movement, is likely to have a different meaning for the individual from the meaning this same act has for people living in the Soviet Union where party membership confers prestige on the member.

Prejudice and society

The research on the authoritarian personality by offering a psychological explanation for prejudice and anti-democratic beliefs has contributed much to the understanding of prejudice and outgroup rejection. But the authors themselves explicitly recognize that, whilst they pinpoint as causes ego-defensive mechanisms linked to childhood experiences, the *content* of attitudes and prejudice derive from society. Their research described how and why certain individuals become *potentially* fascistic and ethnocentric. But precisely because they defer to authority such people are liable to *conform* to societal norms and would project their aggression on outgroups which are already perceived as such in their society. But, if there is a cultural norm of prejudice and discrimination prevalent in a society a great many people (who may well lack all or some of the attributes of the authoritarian personality and who do not have other personal reasons for outgroup hostility) also engage in prejudiced behaviour. Thus, in practice, cultural or societal norms may be much more important than personality in accounting for ethnocentrism, outgroup rejection, prejudice and discrimination. For instance, many people in Germany in Hitler's time became overtly antisemitic who might well not have held such views or voiced them and acted on them in a society in which such attitudes were frowned upon. Equally, in a society in which there is a long-standing prejudice against black people a white person might find it easier to discriminate against black people than not to do so, at any rate in public. The difference between such 'norm-conforming' attitudes and behaviour and 'ego-defensive' attitudes lies not only in their origins — in societal norms or in the psychology of the individual — but in the extent to which they are resistant to change. Ego-defensive attitudes tend to be tenaciously held because they are important to the people who hold them as a defence against aspects of their personalities which they do not want to face consciously. Norm-conforming attitudes, by contrast, respond more readily to new information or experience, reasoned argument or to a change in circumstances.

A study by Minard (1952), described in Box 12, illustrates the interplay between wider socio-cultural attitudes (or, to use a different terminology widely-held social representations) and those held by given individuals, the implication being that the *extent* to which the individual adopts or upholds societal norms is linked to the individual's personality or his or her prior attitudes or other predispositions.

Box 12   Race relations in a coalfield, Minard (1952).

Minard in a study of a West Virginian coal-mining community, demonstrated the interplay of socio-cultural attitudes and attitudes held by individuals which deviated from the prevalent social norms. The norms of this community, at that time, required segregation between black and white people. However, in the mines both racial groups had face-to-face contacts, experienced the same hardships and dangers, did the same work, and achieved the same output. In this situation friendliness and cooperation between the two groups became the social norm and Minard estimated that sixty per cent of the white miners 'integrated' below ground but continued to discriminate against their black colleagues above ground, that is, in both situations they conformed to the prevailing norms for social behaviour. About twenty per cent of the white miners segregated themselves from their black colleagues both above and below ground (that is, they did not adopt the new below-ground-integration norm) and the remaining twenty per cent attempted social integration in both situations (that is, they deviated above ground from the prevailing norms).

The minorities who did not conform to the social norms (above and below ground) may well be assumed to have had personal reasons or attributes which enabled them to resist social pressures to conform to prevailing norms. What this study also illustrates is that for Southern whites of that period it is likely to have been much easier to show friendly behaviour towards black people in circumstances where few other white people can observe their behaviour than to show friendliness in public (above ground).

Pettigrew (1958, 1964) also demonstrated the interplay of personality and socio-cultural factors. He showed that the differences in racial attitudes between the south and the north in the United States reflected the prevailing social norms and that personality tendencies played a role only in a minority of the prejudiced population who manifested extreme expression of prejudice. His research also showed that the more pervasive anti-black attitudes in the south were not partnered by antisemitism or authoritarianism as would be predicted by the theory of the authoritarian personality. Incidentally, we may note that research on race relations before the 1970s always explored the attitudes of white people, the attitudes of black people were ignored. To be charitable one might, of course, accept that, in that earlier period, it was the economically more powerful whites who were in a position to discriminate and that hence the exploration (and change) of their attitudes was more important. But it is not surprising, given that social scientists thought of black/white relations as requiring a change of attitudes among the majority population, that they were unprepared for the rise of the Civil Rights movement in the 1960s 'a situation in which a major part of the initiative for change did not come from the white man but rather from the black' (Coser 1967, p. 148.)

Prejudice, then, may be rooted in the personality or stem from the cultural norms of a society but the two are linked. We have already seen that society may provide ready-made scapegoats in the shape of minority groups onto which prejudiced people can project aggression which they cannot express against those (such as their parents) who frustrated them in the first place. But, assuming the authoritarian personality is the outcome of child rearing practices, then such practices may not only reflect the authoritarian biases of individual parents, but the wider authoritarian values of a society which are perpetuated from generation to generation. The fact that Californians on the whole were not and did not become authoritarians, leave alone fascists, suggests that Adorno and his colleagues tapped a personality type which was fairly rare in that society. By contrast, we might speculate that the fact that the Nazi ideology found ready acceptance in Germany in the 1930s, suggests that it may have been the pre-existing cultural values and social institutions which had produced the parents who were authoritarian and who, in turn, induced a susceptibility to authoritarianism in their children.

Intergroup conflict, however, is not only generated by widely diffused cultural attitudes or by individuals who vent their frustration on convenient minority groups or other scapegoats but by conflict over resources or status (which may reflect long-term inequalities in a society). These issues will be discussed in the next section.

Conflict, competition and incompatible goals

So far we have seen that intergroup conflict may be described as arising from attitudes or personality dispositions which existed *prior* to any subsequent conflict or acts of discrimination between groups. In this section we will review another classic series of studies which, by contrast, shows that negative attitudes towards the outgroup and increasingly positive attitudes towards the ingroup can develop *as a result* of conflict and competition. These studies particularly clearly illustrate this sequence as they investigated groups which started off as equals and without a history of differences behind them. This research was carried out between 1949 and 1953 by an author whose work we have already considered in Section I — Muzafer Sherif, in collaboration with his wife and other social psychologists (Sherif and Sherif, 1953; Sherif *et al.*, 1955; Sherif *et al.*, 1961). Their studies, described in Boxes 13 and 14, are notable not only for their findings and theoretical formulations but for the ingenuity of their methods. They used summer camps for boys who were about twelve years

old as locations for realistic field experiments. The boys w
in the experiments, however, did not know this at the tim
the camp was a genuine summer camp, something
American children, and they thought the researchers we

Box 13   *Ingroups and outgroups (Sherif and Sherif, 1953; Sherif et al., 1955; Sherif et al., 1961.*

Sherif and his colleagues started by inviting twenty-two boys to a summer camp. The boys came from similar backgrounds but did not know each other until they met in the camp. Two separate groups were formed by allocating the boys to two different cabins. The boys engaged in the usual camp tasks and activities which required their cooperation within their own group. The purpose of the first week was to study the evolution of group norms and of a group structure in each of the groups. It was noted, not unexpectedly, that the boys in each group became friendly with each other and that a strong ingroup feeling developed. In one experiment, Sherif deliberately split up boys who had become friendly with each other at the camp within their original groups into new separate groups. Quickly, new ingroup relations were again established and within a few days they ignored previous friends and instead chose as friends members of their new groups.

In these studies, once two distinct groups had been formed, the groups were brought into contact in competitive and frustrating conditions, designed to create conflict between the two groups; specifically, matters were arranged so that the success of one group in games or other camp activities inevitably meant defeat for the other, that is, the goals of the two groups were, and were seen as, incompatible.

What were the consequences? Quite quickly *unfavourable attitudes and stereotypes* developed about the members of the *other group* and the boys did not want to have anything to do with those in the other group even though they did not differ in background and had been matched closely in physical and personal characteristics.

A second consequence was the *over-evaluation of the ingroup* and a strengthening of self-justifying attitudes towards one's own group. Cooperation increased within the group (though one group deposed its demoralized leader) and *animosity towards the outgroup* also increased.

Sherif and his colleagues then explored how to reduce the hostile attitudes and behaviour of each group towards the other.

Box 14   *The reduction of hostile attitudes and behaviour (Sherif and Sherif, 1953; Sherif et al., 1955; Sherif et al., 1961.*

A number of situations were arranged where both groups met whilst engaged in enjoyable activities — they watched a film, had lunch together, and so on. However, this strategy did not lead to a decrease in the existing intergroup hostility. The boys used these situations to exchange invectives and behave aggressively. The competition between the groups, even though it had lasted only one week, guided their views of each other. Sherif and his colleagues concluded that *mere contact*, without regard to the conditions of contact, will not of itself reduce unfavourable intergroup attitudes and behaviour.

The experiment was, therefore, taken a step further and various *superordinate goals* were introduced to overcome the effects of the incompatible goals which separated the two groups. Superordinate goals are defined as goals which cannot be reached by the efforts and resources of one group alone but require the coordinated efforts and resources of both groups. Such situations were deliberately engineered, for instance, the camp's water supply was 'sabotaged' and had to be repaired with everyone's help, and the camp truck was made to break down some miles from the camp and was eventually pulled to the camp by all twenty-two boys using a tug-of-war rope.

Through these cooperative activities, forced on the boys by the needs of the situation, hostility and unfavourable stereotypes were indeed reduced. This happened not as a result of any one event, but over a period of time during which the boys mixed more freely, became more friendly with each other and eventually travelled home peacefully in the same bus.

What conclusions can we draw from this series of experiments?

First, as we already know from earlier sections in this book, groups are formed when people have the opportunity to interact and become inter-dependent.

Second, intergroup hostility and discrimination can be engineered through competition between two groups and such competition increases positive ingroup evaluation, rejection of the outgroup and conflict between the groups. Hostile attitudes and behaviour, in this viewpoint, are seen to *follow* from the situation thus created, not the other way round — another instance, perhaps, of the reduction of cognitive dissonance where attitudes and beliefs are aligned with the behaviour already engaged in. But, intergroup behaviour here is specifically seen not as based on the original attitudes of individuals, but as 'grounded' in 'the social facts' (Durkheim, 1897, 1950) of competition or cooperation resulting from group membership. It is the incompatibility of group interests and goals which causes intergroup hostility and conflict according to this view.

Third, communications and contacts between hostile groups, rather than improving matters, become occasions for recrimination and hostility *unless* superordinate goals are established which have compelling objectives for all concerned and which can only be reached by their cooperation. One might also think that 'superordinate' ideologies (such as 'what is important is playing the game, not winning') could reduce or prevent conflict. But perhaps, American schoolboys have not been exposed to this particular ideology, or the experimental situation, as we have seen before, exerted overwhelming pressures on the participants.

Fourth, superordinate goals, in this case at any rate, lead to the dissolution of the two separate groups and the formation of a single 'superordinate' group as a result of all the boys jointly overcoming the difficulties they all faced. This is reminiscent of times of war when greater social cohesion can be achieved (though in Britain after the Second World War the class struggle re-emerged and became again a focal point in the elections of 1945). The resolution of industrial conflict, too, depends on both employers and employees recognizing the superordinate goal of their continued existence.

To recapitulate: the main lesson to be learnt from these studies (and which can be applied to many contemporary issues) is that outgroup rejection arises out of real conflict. Once the ingroup and outgroup are formed and perceived as such, hostile attitudes are generated and communications and contacts between the groups become hostile in tone or cease and this severance of positive interactions may further increase the conflict and the hostile attitudes and perceptions. If we accept that real conflict such as competition for jobs and housing, causes the negative attitudes one group may have for another then one might suggest that the best remedy for racial antagonism or for other divisions in society is the creation of full employment and prosperity. Without these, people will see themselves as competing for jobs, for housing and other scarce resources. In such conditions of competition and conflict one defence mechanism available to them is to project negative feelings on to those who can readily be identified as an outgroup for contemporary or historical reasons and to enhance the evaluation of and ingroup feeling for their own group. Here, too, then we arrive at the same defence mechanism as we did previously — but its genesis is different. Conflict here is seen as giving rise to hostile attitudes and behaviour. Previously we saw that prior negative attitudes — whether such attitudes are norm-conforming, ego-defensive or, indeed, both at the same time — can lead to discrimination and conflict. We can readily see that these explanations are not mutually exclusive in that negative attitudes towards a group may generate conflicts which then, in turn, may increase feelings and attitudes of hostility towards that group. Sherif's research is striking because his boys on arrival in the summer camp neither had hostile predispositions nor did they have any group affiliations which designated boys in other groups as outgroups. In life, in general, we tend to be locked into ready-made groups with ready-made attitudes. Thus conflict between racial groups, or between Muslims and Hindus in India at the time of India gaining independence, or between Catholics and Protestants in Northern Ireland can only be understood in terms of the history of these societies or groups. It no longer matters whether, initially, conflict gave rise to attitudes, or attitudes generated conflict. But, from the point of view of social psychological theory and the insights it can provide, it is worthwhile to demonstrate the interplay between attitudes and conflict.

Before leaving Sherif's summer camps it is worth mentioning a recent study carried out in Britain which set out to challenge some of the conclusions reached by Sherif and his colleagues. These British researchers (Tyerman and Spencer, 1983) hold that the Sherifs' findings arise from the transitory nature of their experimental groups. They hypothesize that competition between groups is *not a sufficient condition* for the rise of hostile deeds and attitudes and increased ingroup solidarity. In their own study they observed boy scouts, who had regularly interacted with each other during the year, at their annual camp. Many of their activities were similar to those carried out by the boys at Sherif's camp and the scout group was divided into four 'patrols' who competed with each other in situations which were familiar to them from previous camps. The authors found support for their hypothesis. Friendship ties which had been formed before the boys arrived at the camp were maintained across the divisions into patrols; competition remained friendly; and ingroup solidarity showed no increase. The authors argue that their results reflect the fact that the four patrols continued to see themselves as part of the whole (superordinate) group, a view which was deliberately fostered by the camp leader. Furthermore, throughout the fortnight at the camp, the boys had opportunities to mix easily at camp fires and outings. This study does not disprove the findings of Sherif but it usefully demonstrates that the motivation of the boys, the spirit in which the subgroups (patrols) compete and the context (the familiarity with camp life, the long-term relationships between the boys and the tone set by the leader) affect the outcome and hence that competition alone is not necessarily a sufficient condition for conflict and hostility between groups.

In the next section we shall explore a further theoretical position which holds that discrimination towards another group may occur in the absence of prior hostile attitudes and in the absence of real conflict between groups and that such behaviour may be triggered off by the mere *perception* of the existence of two groups.

The minimal group

The suggestion that the arbitrary division of people into groups is a sufficient condition for discriminatory behaviour to occur is based on the work of Tajfel and his colleagues (Tajfel *et al.*, 1971; Billig and Tajfel, 1973; Tajfel, 1978; Tajfel and Turner, 1979). They argue that before any discrimination can occur there must be a categorization of people as members of ingroups and outgroups. However, the novel point they make (and which their experiments support) is that the very act of categorization *by itself* leads to intergroup behaviours which discriminate against the outgroup and favour the ingroup (Tajfel *et al.* 1971). In their experiments they were able to isolate social categorization from variables such as friendship or a common purpose or task in which group members might be involved. They eliminated face-to-face contact, conflict of interests, the possibility of any previous hostility or any utilitarian or instrumental link between subjects' responses and their self-interest. What they did was to create artificial groups among fourteen/fifteen year old comprehensive schoolboys in Bristol.

These 'minimal' groups which were bereft of all the features which normally characterize intergroup relations were formed on the basis of arbitrary and superficial criteria (for instance, the toss of a coin or the preference the boys expressed for the reproduction of one of two paintings), or, indeed, on a completely random basis (Billig and Tajfel, 1973) so as to eliminate the explanation that 'perceived similarity' among group members was responsible for the outcome of these experiments. Nevertheless, when individual group members, working on their own in separate cubicles, were given the opportunity of behaving in ways which would benefit other anonymous, unknown and unseen members of their own group (all they knew was that they *were* members of their own group) to the detriment of the members of the other group by awarding more points or other rewards to members of their 'own' group, this opportunity was frequently taken. This was so even when in some of the experiments a non-discriminatory or cooperative strategy would have maximized the outcome for ingroup members. There was evidently a desire to maximize the *differentials* between the group (the better to set each group apart from the other) even when there was no other reason for competitiveness.

Setting oneself off against others is quite a common experience in life. Thus, if you are a wage or salary earner, your satisfaction with the level of your renumeration may derive, at least in part, not from its absolute amount but from the differentials established between your income and that of those who earn less. You may be able to justify your view that a person of your skill or educational level or experience should earn more than those with less education, training or experience (though such justifications can be argued against) but in the 'minimal group' experiments

there was no meaningful criterion for setting oneself off again:t others
except the arbitrary division into groups. We are faced here with expe-
rimenter-created definitions of the situation where the subjects have no
opportunity to examine the basis of the division or to gain information on
the members of their own group or of those of the outgroup. However, the
fact that the subjects are given only minimal information — mere categorization — does not invalidate the findings, on the contrary, it makes
them all the more startling and thought provoking (though the very artificiality of the situation requires caution in extrapolating from these
experiments to other situations). *If* ingroup membership had not mattered
to these boys, they would have allocated points and rewards at random
(although once they started by rewarding ingroup members, this might
have been the beginning of a 'response norm' as we noted in discussing
experiments using the autokinetic effect.

What psychological processes are likely to be at work here? Tajfel and
Turner suggest:

> Two points stand out: first, minimal intergroup discrimination is not based
> on incompatible group interests; second, the baseline conditions for inter-
> group competition seem indeed so minimal as to cause the suspicions that
> we are dealing here with some factors or process inherent in the intergroup
> situations itself (1979, pp. 39—40).

I have previously mentioned Festinger's theory of social comparison
processes which proposes that *individuals* compare themselves with
others in order to establish or validate their behaviour or attitudes, particularly where 'objective' criteria are lacking. Tajfel and Turner (1979)
argue that an equivalent process takes place in *groups* and that every
group needs to maintain a positive social identity *vis-à-vis* other social
groups.

They conceive of groups as a collection of individuals who *perceive
themselves* to be members of the same social category.[5] They look on social
categorizations as resulting from *cognitive processes* which allow individuals to classify and order the environment and which enable them to
define their own place in society. Social groups hence provide their
members with an identification of themselves in social terms. In this view,
social groups may be conceptualized as a number of individuals who share
a common social identification of themselves (Turner, 1982) and group
behaviour may be conceived as dependent on, and arising from, the func-
tioning of such shared social identifications. Through the process of identifying with a particular group and categorizing oneself as a member, one
may be said to develop a social identity.

In this view, by competing with, and by discriminating against,
members of other groups, individuals can create and maintain a positive
image of their own group, and hence of themselves. This, as Tajfel and his
colleagues have demonstrated, is true even of minimal ephemeral groups

who, perhaps precisely because of the lack of an objective reality, have to engage in social comparisons with the other group in order to establish a social identity. Social categorization, identification with a group, the formation of a social identity, enhanced ingroup feeling and discrimination against the outgroup in this view are all part of the same basic cognitive processes. Tajfel and Turner (1979) think that Sherif's work on intergroup behaviour, by focusing on real conflicts between groups, has neglected to explore the processes which lead to ingroup identification in the first place. Sherif, as we have seen, viewed ingroup identification as largely the *consequence* of a real conflict between groups. Tajfel and Turner (1979), by contrast, address themselves to the exploration of the psychological processes which lead to the development of such positive ingroup identification. As we shall see in the next section, their starting point is the distinction between two kinds of social behaviour: *interpersonal* and *intergroup behaviour*, and two kinds of identities: *personal* and *social identity*.

Personal and social identities

Tajfel and Turner (1979) describe, at one extreme of a continuum, *interpersonal behaviour* which is based on purely personal relationships and the characteristics of the interacting individuals, such as those of a pair of close friends or of husband and wife (though they may well have come together because they belonged to the same 'social categories' — class, neighbourhood, firm or club). But, even in these intensely personal relationships, once they cease to be wholly satisfactory, quarrels or abuse tend to be in terms of social categories — 'just like a woman' or 'I cannot stand your lower middle class attitudes'. Of course, where people use such social categories, it may be because they are afraid to make a quarrel too personal. It is easier and less final, to say 'just like a woman' than to say 'just like you'.

At the other extreme Tajfel and Turner see *intergroup behaviour* as largely determined by the group memberships of the interacting individuals. Thus, the personal characteristics of a shop steward and a foreman or of members of the CBI and the TUC would *not* be the main determinants of their interactions. Their relationships will be primarily characterized by the positions they will take because of their group memberships and 'mandates' from these groups. The members of the two interacting groups will perceive each other largely in terms of their group memberships, at any rate for the purposes of their professional interaction — even though a senior union leader and a senior management representative may both live in the same 'bourgeois' lifestyle and have personal characteristics in common. Much work on 'communications' has demonstrated that what people say or write in their capacity as spokespersons for their group members or as expert witnesses is usually pre-judged or misinterpreted by their audiences because the recipients of the communication are aware of its source and guard themselves against unwelcome influences or, as the case may be, are the more willing to listen to the message. Indeed this point also arises from our discussion of the influence of minorities.

We have seen that where minorities not only present views which are at odds with those of the majority but where they are categorized as outgroups (double minorities) they have greater difficulty in gaining influence though a flexible style of negotiation enables common ground or, in our present terminology, common category or group membership to be established and perceived. As Mugny *et al.* (1984) argue the acceptance of social influence emanating from a minority implies not only the adoption by the majority of the specific new views proposed by the minority but also some changes in identification. It is precisely because of this that minority influence often fails to achieve manifest change as opposed to latent conversion effects: the psychological cost of publicly identifying with an outgroup is too high given the strong evidence from Tajfel that the fact of categorizing oneself as an ingroup member itself leads to discrimination towards the outgroup. We can see, therefore, that social influence processes, and particularily those coming from a minority group, need to be considered also in the theoretical framework of ingroup identification and intergroup discrimination.

Perceiving people in terms of their group memberships tends to imply a focus on relatively few characteristics which are salient from the point of view of the observer's group. This process of 'stereotyping' simplifies and orders our impressions and perceptions. Without thought or examination we will 'know' the characteristics of people such as 'union leaders' or 'employers' or those of members of a religious or racial or political group since we already have a picture of them based on our attitudes or pre-judices. We attribute to them a 'social identity'. As Berger and Luckman (1967) have argued, social reality is not out there to be simply seen and assimilated but is a *construction* based on preconceptions as well as reflecting the actual events or people which are observed and interpreted. However, stereotyping is not only a cognitive process of simplifying and structuring our social world, it tends to have the function of differentiating ourselves from outgroups and of justifying actions against such groups.

Turner (1982), makes the further point that individuals stereotype *themselves*, a process he refers to as 'depersonalization'. This allows the individual to 'switch on' or emphasize the different social identities he or she has developed as a member of his or her sex, class, occupation or in the role of sportsman, husband or wife, 'friend of the earth'. woman's libber or whatever, when these become salient. Such social identity or identities are distinguished by Turner from personal identity, the latter referring to the personal characteristics and attributes which make the individual unique. Inevitably, social identities are not wholly divorced from one's personal identity; one's experience of a social identity (say that of being a member of a profession or a sect) will affect what one is like 'deep down' — one's personal identity (what one is like 'deep down') will have contributed to one's choice of social identities. The concepts of personal identity and social identity merely highlight that we may behave (and feel) differently in different situations. The concept of *role*, as we have already seen in the study of prisoners and guards, has the same explanatory aim and power.

Turner sees the switch in self-concept from personal to social identity as corresponding to, and responsible for, a shift from interpersonal to intergroup behaviour with its concomitant stereotypic perception both of the members of the ingroup and of those in the outgroup. Do you think of yourself as a Scot as contrasted with an English person? Or as a woman as contrasted with a man? Or as a member of the engineering department as contrasted with members of the sales department? When you think of yourself in such ways do you attribute to yourself certain (limited) characteristics which you think are typical of the Scots, of women, of engineers? If you do, then you are thinking of yourself in terms of your social identities (or, to refer back to concepts we used earlier, to the perceived identities of your reference groups) rather than in terms of your idiosyncratic features as an individual. At times, when such social identities are salient, your interactions will be in terms of your group membership both within your group and towards the outgroup. The crucial statement here is, of course, 'when they are salient'. A fight or an argument between several people may be purely interpersonal. On the other hand, it may have started as or become an intergroup affair because the opponents see themselves as members of two groups — black and white, or picket line and strike breakers — though in other situations the *same* people may interact peacefully or, for that matter, have an interpersonal argument. Thus, even where groups are involved in a conflict, not all occasions when members of such groups meet up with each other are categorized as intergroup situations. However, the longer the history of a conflict or the more intense it is, the more likely is it that any interactions are viewed as 'intergroup' rather than 'interpersonal' encounters. In other words, the long-standing intergroup conflict becomes so salient that it may affect all relationships and encounters. Nevertheless, situational clues are also important. In London, for instance, it is rare for Greek and Turkish Cypriots or for Hindus and Moslems to clash.

Is the distinction between personal and social identities useful beyond the descriptive level? Group membership and, therefore, social identities become salient at times of threat or conflict, as the Sherifs (1953) and many others have demonstrated, or when norms are challenged by new experiences (as Minard's study (1952) of the coal miners' attitudes below and above ground has indicated) or when people are faced by uncertainty or ambiguity (as Asch (1955) has shown). We would, therefore, expect intergroup behaviour to be more hostile or competitive than interpersonal behaviour (and Turner's formulation might alert us to this) and the hostility to be less capable of reduction since hostility towards the outgroup is accompanied by an increased sense of belongingness to the ingroup and the over-evaluation of its members.

Brown and Turner (1981) are also concerned to demonstrate that it is inherently difficult to extrapolate from theories of interpersonal behaviour to the explanation of intergroup behaviour. They criticize two influential positions which have attempted to do so, Rokeach's *belief congruence theory* and so-called *contact theorists*.

They first examine Rokeach's belief congruence theory (Rokeach 1960; 1968) which proposes that the similarity or congruence between the belief systems of individuals is an important determinant of their attitudes towards each other and that similarities and differences between people's beliefs are more important for their mutual acceptance or rejection than their group membership. Specifically, whilst this theory could be applied to discrimination against any outgroup, Rokeach focused on discrimination against racially or ethnically distinct outgroups. Rokeach explains race prejudice as an outcome of perceived or assumed belief incongruence. His research (and that of others, for instance, Byrne (1971) seems to establish that individual white subjects (students from one university in the north and from one in the south of the United States) are usually more attracted to black subjects to whom *similar* beliefs are attributed than to white subjects to whom different beliefs are attributed by the researcher. Brown and Turner point out that belief congruence is a theory of interpersonal attraction and has no implications for explaining prejudice and racism which represent intergroup behaviour and as such tend to follow established social norms for intergroup behaviour. Furthermore, one might add, the findings were obtained in the laboratory (as, indeed were Turner's), away from social contexts and social pressures. Racism and prejudice, however, are *social* problems and not a temporary response in a laboratory by an *individual*. In Rokeach's paradigm people were likely to be perceived as unique individuals and not as members of outgroups. In consequence, a person may be preferred to another (because he or she holds similar beliefs) without this generalizing to their (racial) outgroup as a whole. Indeed, what subjects in this situation do is to create for themselves a satisfactory social, as well as personal, identity by making the person with similar beliefs a member of their own (reference) group. However, as soon as other aspects become salient to individuals, for instance, in a situation of racial conflict, other attitudes and stereotypical views come to predominate. Thus, it will probably be difficult to get an inter-racial club going in a situation where there has been tension and conflict between racial groups as this will have had the effect of accentuating ingroup evaluation and outgroup rejection (even though the assumption would be that the club serves the needs and interests of several racial groups). In a different sort of emotional climate, however, interpersonal relations, possibly based on belief similarities or common interest, can cut across racial or other divisions precisely because the new group (for instance, a club for keen amateur photographers) becomes more salient than other factors (such as racial divisions) and new norms governing the interpersonal relations in the club will evolve. In such a situation, of course, we may expect belief similarity to develop as a new group norm or, equally likely, members will *assume* that such similarity exists and hence are likely to perceive it.

Secondly, Brown and Turner (1981) also question the underlying assumptions of *contact theorists* that contact between members of different groups, on an equal status basis and backed by wider social norms or legislation, will lead to a reduction in prejudice and discrimination. This view was advocated by Allport (1954) in his seminal book on prejudice, and is reflected, for instance, by Pettigrew (1971), Minard (1952) and Deutsch and Collins (1951).

We have already seen in discussing the experiments of the Sherifs (1953) and their colleagues that *mere contact* heightened rather than reduced intergroup conflict. Deutsch and Collins (1951), however, found that in racially integrated housing estates (a new social initiative when they carried out their research) more and friendlier contacts were made between the members of the different racial groups than in segregated estates (even though all the families lived there only because they had no choice and endeavoured to move as soon as they could). However, the matter is not so simple. Was there a *general* reduction in prejudice by white people or did the improved attitudes relate only to specific black neighbours? Would these new attitudes persist (become 'internalized' in Kelman's phrase) if people moved away? If they did persist, would the effect be due to contact with their black neighbours or to a more general change which took place at the same time in the norms of the wider society in the wake of new laws or education or improved employment prospects? We have already noted that Minard (1952) found reductions in prejudice at the workplace where they were sanctioned by unions and employers, but not to the same extent in the wider community where segregation was still usual. Amir (1969) points out that interracial attitudes were improved markedly when blacks and whites served side by side in battle or on ships during the Second World War (though their relationships at base camp were not so good). Thus, personal contact, superordinate goals and the sharing of dangers seem to have contributed to improved relationships.

Brown and Turner (1981) in discussing contact theorists make the point that intergroup contact *can* reduce conflict or prejudice but not because it encourages *interpersonal* friendships (as Deutsch and Collins might argue) but because contact changes the nature and structure of the *intergroup* relationship. Hence, in fact, whilst analytically distinct, there may be a continuum between interpersonal and intergroup behaviour, just as there is also a continuum between personal and social identities.

In conclusion, we need to note that in real life it may not usually be possible to establish whether discriminatory intergroup behaviour is based on 'real' conflict or on attempts to achieve distinctiveness for one's own group. This is so because, outside the laboratory, distinctiveness for one's own group tends to be achieved by setting oneself apart from those others who are already in some sense different from oneself or one's group. Whether these differences are between the skilled and the unskilled, the Scots and the English or black and white people, once these categorizations and distinctions have been made they tend to become 'institutionalized' and part of the culture and ideology of these groups. Where there are tangible economic reasons for continuing them they tend to be even more difficult to dislodge and the economic differences may, of course, be the result of long-term discrimination.

If competition with, and discrimination against, the outgroup encourage positive ingroup feelings (and this is something people apparently value) can ingroup feelings be achieved in socially acceptable ways, for instance, by peaceful competition in sport, particularly in team sports, or through competition between work teams or between school 'houses'? The difficulty with this line of reasoning is two-fold. One, the psychological satisfaction of ingroup belongingness seems almost inevitably also to lead to stereotypic and hostile perceptions of the outgroup and it is difficult to strike a healthy balance. Two, and equally or even more important, there may come a point where the participants in opposing groups or teams can see that they are being exploited. Thus in industry, *group incentives*, where people are interdependent on each other or where there is competition between several teams, tend to work better than *individual incentives* (in terms of output *and* job satisfaction) but only so long as both management and workers share the same perceptions and agree that increased productivity (their joint superordinate goal) is what they all aspire to. Once they do not, for instance when workers believe that increased output will lead to rate cutting or unemployment, incentives, whether based on individual or group effort, tend to cease to have any effect at all.

Superordinate goals may be effective in eliminating conflicts between groups *within* a society; it would also appear that diverse groups can be rallied to the same cause if a target group *outside* the immediate situation or the society can be identified. Such is the paradox of human nature and society that the obscenity of war can be a psychologically uplifting experience: a socially acceptable outgroup (outside one's own country) is identified and ingroup feeling is enhanced. In Freudian terms, as you will know from our discussion of ego-defensive attitudes, aggression can be directed towards and displaced onto a socially sanctioned target without arousing the guilt feelings which so often accompany aggression against other targets such as members of one's own family.

In discussing intergroup conflict, we cannot avoid being aware of the conflict going on within our own country in Northern Ireland. Cairns (1982) has used Tajfel's and his colleagues' distinctions between personal and social identity and between interpersonal and intergroup behaviour to analyse the situation and the perceptions and feelings of people in Northern Ireland. He points out that social identity there is defined in terms of Protestant and Catholic and that 'potentially cross-cutting categories such as sex or class are relatively unimportant' (p. 281). He further points out that the cues — residence, accent, first and last names, schools attended and appearance — which enable people to recognize who is or is not a member of their own religious group are learned in childhood and, whilst superficially not as obvious as racial differences, are well understood and used. These social categorizations and the concomitant experience of distinct and non-overlapping group memberships produce a strong sense, and a high level of awareness, of social identity and a strong emotional investment in this identity. As Tajfel has pointed out, to maintain a positive social identity, one needs to engage in social comparison processes with an outgroup. Such comparisons, in the context of the long-standing economic, political and religious differences in Northern Ireland, will almost inevitably lead to the intensification of existing distinctions and an emphasis on the differences between the groups. As Cairns points out, whilst these processes enable each group to have a positive and distinct identity, this very outcome adds to the historical, economic and other divisions existing in Northern Ireland society a psychological mechanism which perpetuates these divisions.

Is intergroup conflict inevitable?

The work of Tajfel and his colleagues seems to demonstrate quite conclusively that people value group membership *per se* and that, to experience a positive social identity their own group must be capable of differentiation from other groups. This, in turn, has in their experiments lead to discrimination against members of the outgroup because such discriminatory strategies will establish a distinction between the ingroup and the outgroup and this process enhances a positive social identity.

But are these results inevitable? The generality of the phenomenon has been examined in laboratory studies in England and in Europe with, on the whole, results which confirm the original findings and Cairn's analysis suggests that Tajfel's theory applies to Northern Ireland. But a study which took place in New Zealand (described in Box 15) shows the effect of different cultural values.

Box 15   'Cross-cultural studies of minimal groups' (Wetherall, 1982).

Wetherall showed that the discriminatory behaviour found in the 'minimal' group situation can be influenced by cultural norms, an explanation which had previously been discounted and rejected by Tajfel and his co-workers. Wetherall conducted a series of 'minimal' group experiments with Polynesian and white children in New Zealand schools. She found that both groups displayed ingroup bias in the allocation of rewards but that the Polynesian children moderated their discrimination, displaying greater generosity to the outgroup. She explains these findings by pointing out that Polynesians in New Zealand had maintained their native cultural institutions which are based on cooperation, particularly among members of the extended family. A person's status among Polynesians is associated with the extent of his or her generosity. For Polynesians to distinguish themselves and their group from others may, therefore, in such experiments as well as in real life, depend on being generous to them (rather than, as did the European groups, discriminate against them). Thus, the cultural values and norms of these children (contrary to Tajfel's original expectations) influenced their behaviour towards the outgroup in the experimental situation.

We might speculate, therefore, that discrimination towards outgroups is not inevitable, *provided* we can learn to be more cooperative and to change our social institutions and structures to encourage cooperation rather than competition. Whilst Wetherall alerts us to the possibility that discrimination towards another group is not inevitable we nevertheless see the operation of prejudice and discrimination towards minority racial or ethnic groups in many societies. In the next section we will consider an aspect of race relations which social psychologists have explored and that is the impact prejudice and discrimination may have on the self-concept and achievement of minority group children. In other words, this kind of research does not so much seek explanations for the *origins* of prejudice and discrimination but explores their *effects* on children.

Identity formation and achievement of minority group children

Many studies, both in the U.S.A. and in Britain (since large-scale immigration started here in the 1950s) have examined the effects on children of belonging to a racially distinct minority group. A very early study in the United States (Clark and Clark, 1947) used projective methods which involved children making choices among white or black dolls in response to such questions as which doll looked most like the child or which doll did the child want to play with, and so on. One finding in this study which has also emerged later to a greater or lesser extent in other American and British studies using such methods (for a review see Milner, 1984) is that black children preferred the white or light-skinned dolls in response to most such questions. There are though significant age differences and this tendency is more pronounced in younger children. These findings have been interpreted as suggesting that these children do not identify with their own racial group because they have come to have confused feelings about themselves as a consequence of the low status they perceive their own group to have. They may have absorbed the knowledge that it is better to have a white skin than a black one. Yet there is something incongruent about this interpretation since it is the younger children whose main experience must have been in the shelter of their own home environment and who have not yet been exposed to the tougher environment of the wider society who make more of the white doll choices. Even more speculative is the inference drawn that low self-esteem would have deleterious effects on the children's ability to do well at school. The Clarks' findings came from their study of black children in segregated southern schools and in both (de facto) segregated and non-segregated northern schools and was cited as evidence in a series of law cases to press the view that segregated facilities were inherently unequal and therefore unconstitutional. But, in fact, there were no significant differences between the children in the northern mixed schools and those in the southern segregated schools in either their knowledge of racial differences or in their racial identifications. (For a review of the 'desegragation debate' and the role played by social psychologists in bringing about a change in the law, see Murphy *et al.*, 1984).

It is difficult to tease out the meaning of such studies. Some have focused on self-esteem, others on achievement at school. But, even if both these factors had been studied together over a period of time in the same group of children, it would still be inadequate to analyse them as if they were divorced from other experiences the children had in the wider society, the home or their peer groups. We would need to know which of these social settings had proved to be important to the child and had come to be internalized. We also do not know whether unpleasant experiences or the weight of 'racism' will lead to low self-esteem or, on the contrary, to stronger identification with the child's own racial group and rebellion and rejection of the wider white society. When children of West Indian immigrants do not always do as well in British schools as one would expect, then this may be the consequence of rejection of what the wider society has to offer rather than of low self-esteem. All one can say is that projective studies, like the Clarks' research, explore a psychological strand in intergroup relations by looking not at the individual's self-esteem in isolation but by studying it in relation to the child's group memberships. Recent

American and British experience points to a stronger black ingroup identification and from this is likely to grow a positive social identity. Indeed some recent studies have shown that neither here nor in the United States do black children misidentify themselves to the extent they did in the earlier studies (see, for instance, Hraba and Grant (1970) which was based on the original Clark and Clark (1947) study).

However, as we have seen in discussing the psychological climate prevailing in Northern Ireland, positive ingroup identification may bring in its wake satisfactions for the members of the group but it poses problems for intergroup relations. To create an equitable multi-racial and multi-cultural society will not be easy unless different groups perceive themselves as equal in status whilst distinct on some value dimensions. The former is important to minimize over-evaluation of the ingroup and under-evaluation of the outgroup.

The so-called Swann Report (Education for All, 1985) addresses the problem of how to provide an education which meets the needs of the multi-cultural and multi-racial society Britain has become. The impetus for this five-year long study came from the evidence of under-achievement in school by children from certain minority groups, particularly children of West Indian and Bangladeshi descent. By contrast other groups, notably Pakistani children, did as well as the majority children. The Committee, however, was not able to unravel the facts behind these broad statistics since its proposals for a factual survey of the social circumstances of successful and unsuccessful pupils in each ethnic group met with such resistance that they had to be abandoned (as the 'blame' might be put on the children's families). An earlier interim report in 1981, too, aroused hostility as it seemed to focus on the unconscious prejudice of teachers who might, in consequence, expect too little of minority pupils and thus hinder their progress. Inspite of this lack of adequate research, the Committee offers tentative explanations and makes over sixty recommendations. It suggests that many ethnic minority children suffer from an *extra* element of social and economic deprivation over and above that experienced by children in white families of similar socio-economic status. This additional handicap is attributed to discrimination in housing and employment. These disadvantages are thought to account for some of the observed underachievement and will need remedying. The Committee also recommends changes in teacher education and in-service training to bring about a greater awareness of the needs of minority children. The Committee further recommends changes in the curriculum to make it less 'Anglocentric' so that it meets not only the needs of minority pupils but also the needs of the majority who are faced with a changing society. It is hoped that over a period of time, these changes in the curriculum will contribute to a shift in wider social attitudes. In this context, the main Report discusses *racism* and *racist attitudes*, that is, conscious or unconscious attitudes and practices — in schools and elsewhere — which are likely to disadvantage minority groups. The brief overview which was published simultaneously with the main Report shrinks from using these terms and hence perhaps from facing this issue. Alternatively, these words were not used as this Report, like the research reported earlier in this section, was unable to disentangle the precise contributions to and interactions between socio-economic factors, family structure and expectations, teachers' attitudes and 'institutional' racism.

A counterpart to the issue of which group one is to identify with is the issue of who to include in one's own group. This question is implicit in another research tradition which examines the conditions under which people are prepared to come to the assistance of a stranger who needs help. This research field has been given the label of bystander apathy and is discussed in the next section.

Bystander apathy

We saw earlier how easy it is to establish ingroups and outgroups in the laboratory and that these divisions need not stem from historical events, present attitudes or 'real' conflicts between groups. The mere division of people into groups on a quite arbitrary basis can lead to discrimination against those not perceived as of one's own group, though Wetherall's research in New Zealand showed that cultural norms may temper this tendency. But the question 'who do you include in your group?' is one we need to explore further. I have raised this very same question when discussing Milgram's experiments on obedience. It is all very well to 'explain' the findings by stating that the subjects obeyed authority. But, *why* did they do this and *why* was the 'victim' considered an outsider to whom no compassion was owed? Perhaps we can gain some insight into these questions by considering the following real event and the research it generated.

Kitty Genovese was murdered in 1964 in Queens, one of the five boroughs which make up New York City. She was on her way home from a night job in the early hours of the morning when she was stabbed repeatedly over an extended period of time. Thirty-eight residents of this respectable New York City neighbourhood admitted to having witnessed at least part of the attack but none went to her aid or called the police until after she was dead. This 'bystander apathy', as it came to be called, caught the imagination and concern of social psychologists and provided the impetus for more than a decade of research which explored the conditions in which a bystander comes to offer assistance to or withholds it from an unknown person who needs help unexpectedly. In other words, in what sort of circumstances and through what sort of psychological processes will a bystander come to include a stranger into his or her ingroup and offer help? Initially, the focus of research was on the determinants of *non*-intervention, starting with the research by Latané and Darley (1970) which is reported in their book *The Unresponsive Bystander: Why Does He Not Help?* Later the emphasis switched to understanding *altruism* and helping behaviour in crises or emergencies.

Altruism might be defined in terms of acts that objectively provide no benefit to and often cause harm or distress to the actor while benefiting another. However, strictly speaking, such selfless acts may nevertheless be rewarding to the actor in the sense that people may be living up to the self-image they have of themselves as caring persons. Freud also pointed out that apparently altruistic acts are a form of defence against aggressive impulses which need to be kept in check to aid a person's self-esteem.

In the context of research on bystander apathy, helping behaviour in crises or emergencies tends to be seen as the intervention by the amateur or bystander rather than the help or assistance given by the pro-fessional — doctor, nurse, police or firefighter — who are formally and professionally required to give help.

Psychologists have asked many questions about bystander intervention or apathy. What processes are at work which lead to an individual's decision to go to the aid (or not) of someone else in an emergency? How do individuals *perceive* such situations, how do they *feel* in the situation, how do they judge the *victim*, how do they assess the *costs* of intervention?

However, here we can only focus on two aspects of this more general phenomenon — one, how is ingroup feeling generated between the victim and the bystander? And, two, how is this process affected by the presence of other bystanders — does such a presence lead to ingroup feelings between the bystanders rather than between the bystander and the victim? See Box 16.

Box 16   *Research on bystander apathy, Latané and Darley (1968) and Latané and Rodin (1969).*

In their first study, Latané and Darley used an experimental situation which involved the subjects hearing someone apparently having a severe epileptic-like fit in another room. In the experimental room subjects (who had been enlisted to take part in an ostensibly quite dif-ferent research project) found themselves either alone or with four other subjects. The results were quite unequivocal — those subjects who were alone when the victim (apparently) had a seizure in the next room were much more likely to go to his aid and, on average, reacted in less than one-third of the time as compared to those subjects who were in the company of others.

Epileptic fits are perhaps not very common events and so Latané and Rodin (1969) set up a further study in which subjects heard someone (apparently) fall off a ladder in the next room and moan.

The experiment was carried out under four conditions: subjects were —
(a) alone;
(b) two friends were together;
(c) two strangers were together;
(d) the subject was with an experimenter's confederate instructed not to intervene.
Seventy percent of subjects who were alone responded to the situation within sixty-five seconds. Two friends together did nearly as well. When two strangers were together fewer of them reacted and their reaction was much slower. Those subjects who were in the presence of the passive collaborator of the experimenter showed the least and the slowest reaction.

Latané and Darley (1970; 1976) suggested that the presence of other bystanders can affect an individual's response to an emergency in three ways.

First of all, the presence of others may allow the *responsibility* for helping to be diffused among the group (since there are others who could help). Equally, the guilt and blame for not helping may be diffused (and thus the psychological costs to the individual of not helping is reduced).[6]

Second, the reaction of other bystanders to an emergency provides *information* to the individual — thus the passive confederate gives the subject the impression that the situation is less severe than he or she might think.

Third, concern for the evaluation which others might make of him or her *(normative* social influence) can affect a bystander's likelihood of intervention. (The distinction between normative and informational social influence was first explored by Deutsch and Gerrard, 1955.)

Both the second and third point involve social comparison processes. The 'diffusion hypothesis' generated a considerable volume of research. Piliavin *et al.* (1981) who reviewed these studies point out that there is some confusion about this concept. They argue that diffusion of responsibility occurs when responsibility is accepted by the subject but *shared* by all the onlookers. They distinguish 'diffusion of responsibility' from 'dissolution of responsibility' which, they say, occurs when the behaviour of other bystanders cannot be observed and the subject 'rationalizes' that someone else has already helped. Whatever label is attached to the process almost all the studies reveal the inhibitory effect of the presence of others. There is though a limit to such diffusion: Piliavin and his colleagues found in experiments they carried out in the New York subway that help was forthcoming on crowded subway trains as frequently as on relatively empty ones. Perhaps it is more difficult to refuse help in a face-to-face situation. It is also possible that in an enclosed space like a subway carriage a feeling of 'common fate' among the passengers and hence of ingroup membership is generated. The notion, originally proposed by Latané and Darley (1970), that informational social influence, normative social influence and diffusion of responsibility are dynamically distinct processes is upheld by several independent investigations (for instance, by Schwartz and Gottlieb, 1976). Informational social influence primarily affects the bystander's *interpretation* of a situation; diffusion of responsibility occurs later, as does normative social influence which relates to concern about the evaluation by others of one's action, that is, whether one should or should not intervene.

Bystanders, then, have an effect on each other — but do the characteristics of the *victim* also influence the readiness of a bystander to intervene?

As we have already seen in earlier sections it is very easy to engender ingroup favouritism and a feeling of we-ness. Nevertheless, certain factors help to generate such feelings. Many studies found that *similarity* between victim and potential helper and physical *closeness* to the victim arouses sympathy in the bystander and increases the extent to which assistance is forthcoming. The psychological costs for helping a victim should also be less for similar than dissimilar victims as the bystander would be more confident in interacting with a victim who is similar to him or herself in some respects. One implication of this seems to be that the greater the distress or injury, defacement or unusualness of the victims the less are we likely to perceive them as like us and the less help is extended. There is evidence for this point from experiments. For instance, a victim of a (staged) subway emergency who has an unattractive birthmark is less likely to receive help than one who does not have such a mark (Piliavin, Piliavin and Rodin, 1975) and the victim receives more help if he is not bleeding from the mouth than if he is (Piliavin and Piliavin, 1972), presumably because the sight of such 'stigmatized' victims is too horrifying and off-putting, and sympathy is inhibited by defence mechanisms. Other studies show that a stranded motorist who is dressed and groomed neatly is far more likely to receive help than one whose clothing is casual and whose hair is long (Graf and Riddell, 1972).

Since most of the bystander research has been carried out in the United States there are quite a few studies which focus on the effect of race on bystander intervention. Are racially similar victims helped more readily than dissimilar ones? The evidence is inconclusive and Piliavin *et al*. (1981) suggest that, irrespective of their racial attitudes, people may be concerned with projecting a nonbigoted self-image, do not consider themselves as prejudiced (even if they score highly on prejudice on attitude scales) and would hence not easily act negatively towards someone merely on the basis of a person's race. In other words, if white people do not help black people, or vice versa, additional psychological costs (such as loss of self-esteem) may be incurred. Other characteristics of the victim may cross cut with race. Thus, Piliavin, Rodin and Piliavin (1969) varied two victim characteristics: race (black versus white) and source of the problem (illness versus drunkenness) when the victim collapsed in a subway train. Only with the drunk victim was a race effect obtained, not with the apparently disabled victim carrying a cane. They suggest that the costs for not helping were lower for the drunk (since he was perceived as less like oneself, less deserving and his condition as less likely to be serious and indeed self-inflicted) and, in that condition, his race was also weighed in the balance by the potential helper. However, these *post-hoc* explanations for the experimental findings may not be universally true.

Whilst our quick glance at victim — helper interactions has limited itself to exploring the reactions of the casual bystander I cannot resist the temptation to draw your attention to some studies which show that professional helpers, too, distinguish between victims on a variety of criteria and that the help they extend is influenced by how they categorize the victim. For instance, Sudnow (1973) in California and also Simpson (1976) in London show that, if the ambulance crew or the staff in the emergency room think someone is dead or as good as dead, then fewer resuscitation attempts are initiated than if he is categorized as needing help urgently. What category the patient is put in may depend on age. Thus, lack of vital signs of life will be taken at face value if the patient is elderly, the patient will be assumed to be 'dead on arrival' and no attempts at resuscitation will be made. However, the same symptoms in a younger person may be viewed as cardiac arrest, so resuscitation attempts are commenced immediately by the ambulance crew who will race to the hospital and alert the emergency room whilst still on the way.

Simpson (1976) also showed that a patient's presumed moral character may determine the category into which he or she is put. Thus, someone smelling of alcohol (particularly if also shabbily dressed or unwashed), drug addicts, prostitutes, vagrants, persons injured in fights or attempted suicides are less often judged to need urgent attention. Simpson argues that hospital personnel seem to feel that such persons are less deserving of help (just like the drunk person in the subway experiment) than those of a 'higher moral character'. He advises that the best way to survive a heart attack is to 'Look as young as you can, dress well and traditionally, disguise your deviances and keep your breath fresh' (Simpson, 1976, p. 248).

I have in this section from time to time referred to the psychological costs incurred by the helper. But is help always welcome to the victims? Do they incur costs in accepting help? There is, of course, no evidence for answering this question from the studies mentioned here since the situations in which the bystanders' behaviour was observed were all ingeniously faked (in the laboratory or in ecologically more valid settings such as in a subway train or in a street) and there were no genuine victims.

However, we know, for instance from the hostile way in which foreign aid
is often received, that there are psychological costs incurred by the
recipients which need to be hidden from consciousness by directing
hostility rather than thanks towards the provider. In interpersonal relationships, too, we can be embarrassed by two much generosity. 'Exchange
theory' argues that people subjectively evaluate their 'inputs' into a
situation and the 'outcomes' they receive and that they would try to
maintain a balance between the two. Thus we would expect that a victim
receiving help would feel embarrassed at the one-sided and unequal relationship. The same feelings may account for the reluctance of many
people to accept welfare or social work intervention since they cannot
reciprocate the help they receive and which they view, negatively, as
charity or handouts. To stimulate self-help among deprived groups may
in consequence be more effective and less damaging to people's self-
respect.

Conclusions to Section III

I do not want to rehearse here, once more, the arguments and conclusions
outlined in this Section. But, as in my comments at the end of Section I
about the nature of ingroup phenomena and processes, I must stress that
the various explanations advanced here for understanding intergroup
relations and conflicts are not mutually exclusive. Each approach —
whether based on the importance of incompatible goals, on hostile
attitudes and prejudice, on stereotyping and scapegoating, on 'minimal'
groups or on the distinction between and consequences of personal and
social identities — seems to chip away at part only of the unknown. The
important unknown (not just for social psychology but for mankind) is
how we can achieve more inclusive groups or better intergroup relations.
On the one hand, we might think of changes in socialization and
education. Some support for such a view is given by the study of Wetherall
(1982) (page 116). Her work showed that the norms children acquire in
their society guide their reactions to the outgroup. On the other hand, we
need to place these findings against the evidence from other studies mentioned in this book which seem to indicate not only the importance to
people of membership in *small* groups but the enhancement of the psychological pleasure of membership through setting one's own group off
against another. As I pointed out, people seem to manage to feel at one
with large groupings, such as a nation, mainly when there is an external
enemy, which is not a very reassuring conclusion to arrive at if one is
interested in peaceful coexistence.

But, even if the psychological evidence all pointed in the same
direction, most social problems (such as racial prejudice and discrimina-

tion or other intergroup conflicts) cannot be solved at the psychological level alone.

We have seen, for instance, that racial prejudice stems mainly from the norms of a society rather than from the psychological quirks of individuals. Such norms tend to reflect the long-term economic or legal disadvantages which may have created or contributed to the very differences which continue to feed the prejudiced norms.

To change such norms, then, one cannot simply operate on the psychological level and change the content of education or socialization with a view to creating less prejudiced attitudes. Important as this is, one must also change the economic and political position of disadvantaged groups. Thus the legal system of a country will need to provide for and enforce non-discrimination in housing, in job opportunities, in access to education, and so on. The legal framework embodies and defines what a society considers proper and moral and, in turn, will have effects on behaviour (by discouraging discrimination) as well as on the attitudes of the majority and the self-perceptions and social identity of minorities, at least over a period of time. Perhaps we can put this argument another way. Throughout this book we have seen that it is not necessarily the individual who is aggressive to others or unresponsive to their needs but that people may be in situations which allow, or indeed propel them to behave in such a way. This perhaps is the real message of Milgram and Zimbardo. To effect change, then, we need to focus on the social institutions of a society as well as on the attitudes and behaviour of its people.

It is precisely because change needs to proceed on both these fronts, the personal and the social, that intervention is so difficult and is likely to have unintended consequences.

SECTION IV

Are Crowds different from Groups?

In the English language (and presumably in other languages, too) there are words which have an unpleasant or derogatory connotation. Thus 'trade union boss' as compared to 'trade union leader' has nasty overtones and the same can be said of 'capitalist' as compared to 'entrepreneur' or 'employer'. The use of the world 'régime' rather than 'government' is always intended to suggest repression or illegality and 'propaganda' tends not to be equated with 'education'.

'Crowds' in contrast to 'groups' is also one of these emotive terms. It suggests danger, uncontrollable violence, riots, vandalism, lynchings or other apparently irrational behaviours. It has this connotation in part, no doubt, because crowds *can* be destructive and violent but, in part, because a book by Le Bon, published originally in 1895 and still in print, set the scene with a most unflattering analysis of crowd phenomena. Le Bon stressed three characteristics of the crowd: *anonymity* which he sees as leading to irresponsibility; *contagion* by others in the crowd which he sees as leading to a sacrifice of self-interest and of personal standards and to the creation of 'homogeneity' among the members of a crowd; and *suggestibility* which to him implied that the conscious personality had vanished and the 'racial unconscious' had taken over. Many of these alleged attributes of the crowd still inform current research though Le Bon's explanations of the processes operating in the crowd are not necessarily accepted. In particular, contemporary social psychologists would not think of suggestibility in terms of the *racial* unconscious though Freud (1921/1985) suggests that the crowd allows expression of normally *repressed* behaviour (p. 101 in 1985 edition).

Le Bon wrote against the background of the events of the French Revolution but also in the aftermath of the French defeat in the 1870 Franco—Prussian war, the 'insurrection' of the Paris Commune and the rise of socialism in France. His ideas parallel those developed by contemporary sociologists and also those of a later period who basically saw 'mass society' as the result of the breakdown of normal constraints and the crowd as a pathological aggregate of people — a mob — in which individuals lose their identity.

Le Bon's ideas have fascinated many political leaders — Hitler, Mussolini, Stalin, De Gaulle among them. He has also influenced several psychologists. Freud quotes extensively from Le Bon in his wide-ranging analysis of mass phenomena (Freud 1921/1985). Other psychologists, too, have found Le Bon a source of ideas. Crowds, of course, have again become a topical subject in the wake of mass protests and urban riots in many countries since the 1960s and the perceived increase in vandalism and football hooliganism. Several questions therefore pose themselves. Have social psychologists been successful in providing a framework within which such collective actions can be analysed and understood? Do we understand the social contexts in which they occur? Are crowds always hostile or aggressive? Do we have some understanding of what it feels like to be in a crowd, be that a rioting mob or the crowd celebrating New Year's Eve in Trafalgar Square? Can we relate the analysis of crowds to that of groups or to other areas of social psychology? For instance, will be again find evidence of pressures towards conformity or the diffusion of responsibility? Will the concept of 'social identity' help us understand crowd behaviours? Do we understand how crowds come together and how they are mobilized? Do crowds have leaders?

Most writers in using the term crowd refer to a spontaneous, sudden aggregation of people rather than an assembly of people in a predetermined place such as a congregation in church or people attending an advertised political meeting. 'The Times' of June 2nd, 1982, reports: 'The Pope faced a *congregation* of 300,000 . . .' (emphasis added). The *number* of people is, therefore, not necessarily a factor in defining crowds, though the anonymity of the individual amongst a large number of people has often been used as an explanation of crowd behaviour. One of the aspects which has been studied, mainly by sociologists, concerns the speed with which a crowd can be mobilized, for instance, in response to alleged police provocation. The cues and messages and the channels of communication through which potential participants may be alerted are, therefore, also relevant to a description and analysis of a crowd.

However, not all writers limit themselves to spontaneous, initially structureless, assemblies when analysing crowds. Because of the association of the word crowd with collective violence many researchers focus on gangs or similar groupings which have an existence over an extended period of time. Thus the football 'crowd' may consist of rival gangs or rival supporters' groups with their own structures and rituals in which 'aggro' or violence may have a predetermined role. Collective violence may also be a well thought-out strategy in political protest and apparently spontaneous crowds may, in fact, have been carefully brought together, briefed, led and supplied with chants and slogans. As we shall see, social psychologists tend to focus on understanding the psychological changes or processes occurring in people in crowds, whilst sociologists tend to focus on the social contexts in which crowds take actions, spontaneously or otherwise. In the next sections we shall look at some of the studies which have been undertaken to gain an understanding of crowd behaviour and we shall relate these findings to our study of groups.

Deindividuation

For Le Bon the important question was why people in a crowd behave in ways which are uncharacteristic of them as individuals. Fromm, by contrast, sought to understand what motivates some people to submerge their individuality in groups. He thought of individuality and a sense of self-awareness and uniqueness as human attributes which have emerged over a long historical period, a development which, whilst it makes people 'free', may also isolate them from each other and make them fear their freedom (Fromm, 1941).

The concept of deindividuation relates to both these questions. It was Festinger, Pepitone and Newcomb (1952) who, deriving the idea from Le Bon, first postulated the concept of deindividuation which they define 'as a state of affairs in a group where members do not pay attention to other individals *qua* individuals and, correspondingly, the members do not feel they are being singled out by others' (p. 389). Such a state may lead to a reduction of inner constraints for group members and facilitate behaviour which would normally be inhibited. The authors carried out research on laboratory groups, not real crowds, though they expected their findings to throw light on behaviour in crowds. They postulated that groups provide two kinds of satisfaction for their members: at times, satisfaction may derive from one or more individuals being singled out in the group and accorded prestige or status, and hence group membership facilitates ego identity; at other times, satisfaction may be derived from the precise opposite, that is deindividuation or the merging of the individual into the group. Box 17 outlines Festinger *et al.*'s experiment.

Box 17   Deindividuation in a group (Festinger et al. 1952)

Festinger and his colleagues set out to demonstrate the existence of deindividuation by creating a situation in which group members might be tempted to express anti-parent statements (perhaps not quite as common an occurrence in the late 1940s as it may be today). Briefly, the experimenters ran a number of discussion groups for male under-graduate volunteers. They were asked to discuss their own feelings towards their parents after reading a fictitious survey indicating that eighty-seven per cent of a representative student population possessed a strong deep-seated hatred of one or both parents and that those who denied at first that they had such feelings or were reluctant to discuss them were subsequently diagnosed as possessing the most violent forms of hostility. (This latter statement was included to put pressure on members to admit to such feelings and to discuss them.)

Festinger and his colleagues found a correlation between the frequentcy with which negative statements about parents were made and the extent to which their subjects failed to remember who said what in a post-discussion test. They concluded that these results indicated support for their contention that deindividuation leads to a reduction of inhibitions. They found, also, that those groups in which there had been more expression of hostility towards parents were more attractive to their members (as expressed in the willingness to return for further discussions on this topic) and hence that 'submergence' in the group can be thought of as one of the satisfactions to be gained from group membership.

However, one might well argue that deindividuation may *follow* from uninhibited behaviour in groups, rather than be the cause of it. The similarity between group members may increase and less attention be paid to individuals as they engage in unrestrained behaviour. Perhaps because this study by Festinger *et al.* was somewhat unconvincing it took more than a decade before a second was done. Singer, Brush and Lublin (1965) emphasized the importance of internal psychological processes rather than of group membership by defining deindividuation as a 'subjective state in which people lose their self-consciousness' (p. 356). They found in their study that deindividuation led to a larger number of obscene comments being made by their female subjects in conditions of anonymity when discussing pornography and that this increased deindividuation was again complemented by a greater liking for the group.

Zimbardo (1969), in a very influential paper, also focused on the absence of self-awareness and self-evaluation coupled with lowered concern for social evaluation in the state of deindividuation. He saw dein-dividuation as a complex process in which (1) certain situational conditions lead to (2) an internal deindividuated state in which the individual changes his or her perception of him- or herself and of others and (3) engages in relatively uninhibited behaviour whether this is anti-social or 'positive' (such as the expression of intense feelings of happiness or sorrow).

In this paper, Zimbardo, again following Le Bon, proposed *anonymity* as a major source of deindividuation. He was the first to operationalize anonymity by masking and hooding his subjects, a technique frequently copied by later reserchers. He himself, as we have already seen, in a later study hooded the 'prisoners' in his simulated prison.

Zimbardo, however, found it difficult to manipulate anonymity. For instance, in an experiment with troops drawn from the Belgian Army, non-identifiability and loss of personal identity, was again assumed to be created by the soldiers wearing hoods covering their heads. However, the expected results of increased aggression by the deindividuated soldiers was no obtained because the soldiers, unaccustomed as they were to being hooded, became self-conscious, suspicious and anxious. They may have *looked* deindividuated to the experimenter but the results indicated they were not. By contrast, the apparently non-deindividuated subjects in the control group retained the 'normal' extent of deindividuation resulting from their status as uniformed soldiers.

Indeed, uniforms tend to be imposed — in the army, schools, convents, monasteries, prisons or on hospital patients or hospital staff — to reduce individuality. As Goffman (1968, 1971) has so graphically described, we need our personal possessions, including our clothes and room furnishings to present ourselves to the world and to maintain our identity as individuals. Uniforms, then, may increase deindividuation (but they may also assist team effort by presenting a symbol of the common endeavour which binds the group together).

Zimbardo's studies were followed by a considerable number of others but, as Diener (1980) points out, the experimental evidence remains inconclusive and the manipulaton of anonymity at times interacts with other variables in unpredictable ways. This should not surprise us if we accept Zimbardo's view, outlined above, that deindividuation involves prior conditions, a state of mind and the resulting behaviour. Deindividuation is a matter of degree, whichever aspect of this tripartite concept we focus on.

It would appear, then, that the notion of deindividuation, whether or not it arises from anonymity, does not help us very much with understanding behaviour in crowds. Since we are discussing *crowds* in the context of attempting to understand *groups* we may well ask whether the concept of deindividuation applies to the analysis of processes in groups? In discussing the effects of group membership, I have not used this concept (nor does anyone else seem to use it in this context). We might think that any degree of even routine conformity to group norms could be categorized (or castigated) as being due to a lack of self-awareness, or as involving the loss of some individuality or self-regulation. These terms, as I have pointed out, have all been used to describe deindividuation. The reason why deindividuation has not entered the vocabulary of the study of groups is probably due to the compartmentalization of social psychological research but possibly also due to the fact that the notion of deindividuation came on to the scene when a vocabulary of group phenomena was already well established.

There is also, of course, a somewhat different emphasis when social psychologists study groups and when they study deindividuation. In the former case, they seek to explore how individuals can adapt to a group, maintain their individuality and escape from conformity pressures. In the latter case, psychologists accepted, perhaps more readily, that group membership could imply a loss of individuality and sought to explore the precise conditions in which it occurred. However, as we have seen, the first researchers who used the term deindividuation (Festinger *et al.*, 1952) were aware of these complex interactions between the individual and his or her group and emphasized that identification with the group may strengthen ego identification in certain circumstances, and in others it may reduce it and the self become deindividuated and 'submerged' in the group.

There is also the question of how and why people get themselves into situations of deindividuation (apart from laboratory experiments to which they are lured by some cover story). Certainly, sometimes membership of groups may be sought out actively by individuals who seek to lose their inhibitions by joining therapy groups of one kind or another (although this may be partnered by the desire to emerge with a new personality or individuality).

Others may immerse themselves in drug taking sessions or a riot or participate in short term transgression of cultural norms by 'letting go' at an office party, a carnival or in tribal ceremonies leading to a state of trance. Other people may seek longer term solutions to their problems of identity and individuality and become monks or soldiers or join a mass movement (though, of course, other motives also play a part in making such choices).

There is another aspect to deindividuation. Victims of aggression are often 'dehumanized' by starving them, shaving their heads and dressing them in ridiculous and ill-fitting clothes so that they appear less human, and therefore can be transgressed against more easily. Anyone who has ever seen photographs of Nazi concentration camp inmates will appreciate this point. Even the Allied troops who liberated the camps found it difficult to relate to the skeleton-like inmates they found there. Another method of deindividuation or dehumanizing target groups or victims is by developing hostile stereotypes about them which then prevent one from relating to such people as individuals, be they enemies in a war or members of a minority group in one's own country.

An aside can be added here to our earlier discussion of 'mininal groups'. You will recall that in these experiments subjects discriminated in favour of anonymous ingroup members and against equally anonymous outgroup members. Anonymity was deliberately imposed so that individual differences would not influence the reactions of the subjects. From our present context we can see that such depersonalization by imposing

anonymity is only a step away from dehumanizing the 'enemy' so that he
or she can be better discriminated against.

Anonymity, as we have seen, does not necessarily lead to deindividuation nor can we simply use these concepts in an analysis of crowd
phenomena. As Reicher (1984) points out in his study of the troubles in the
St. Paul's area of Bristol in 1980 members of crowds often know each
other and are not anonymous to their immediate neighbours in the crowd.
However, crowds may resent the anonymity of their opponents. Figure 12
shows paragraphs which appeared in *The Times* in a report on some disturbance in the Nothing Hill area of London under the title 'Fireproof
uniforms anger blacks'.

Did such anonymity have an effect on the behaviour of the police? We
do not know but the newspaper report suggests that it did have an effect on
the perceptions and attitudes of some of the West Indians on the scene and
hence may have been a factor in escalating violence.

The concept of deindividuation does not seem particularly appropriate
to an explanation of crowd behaviour (even though it gives some
explanation of why people may behave in uncharacteristic ways in carefully devised laboratory experiments). Thus, some American studies of

> But at least one serious issue is likely to be raised as a result of the disturbance, that of the flameproof suits worn by the 100 officers, including some from the Special Patrol Group, who took part in the action. That uniform, combined with a hard helmet and visor, does not include a police serial number, making it difficult for anyone who wishes to identify and complain against an individual officer to pursue a grievance.
>
> A middle-aged West Indian, who refused to give his name, but who was in the Mangrove restaurant when it was raided, said yesterday: "When they came through the door they looked like zombies, dressed in full black with headgear. All they had was one small stripe saying 'police' on it. We could not know in the world who they were, their faces were covered and they had helmets."

*FIGURE 12.   Excerpt from a report by David Hewson in The Times,
April 22nd, 1982, p. 2 titled 'Fireproof uniforms anger blacks'.*

riots in Watts in Los Angeles in 1965 clearly show that some people join in to be *noticed*, to become aware of their identity, to feel important (Milgram and Toch, 1969) and hence deindividuation would put the wrong label on their motives and experiences.

One might even argue that the concept of deindividuation is unnecessary because there are other established concepts such as roles which fit some of the experiments and observations carried out in an effort to understand deinviduation. For instance, the study discussed earlier (page 85) by Zimbardo and his colleagues (Zimbardo *et al.*, 1973) in which they set up a simulated prison where subjects were allocated at random to the contrasting roles of 'prisoner' and 'guard' is often referred to in the context of deindividuation research. But, although the authors refer to a loss of personal identity and use the word deindividuation, they do so almost as an afterthought. They describe the prisoners and guards as adopting *roles* and the concept of role which relates actual behaviour to prior expectations of what is appropriate in a given context seems much more useful in accounting for the startlingly different behaviours the 'prisoners' and the 'guards' adopted.

The concept of role embodies at least three notions. *One*, it refers to norms, expectations, taboos or responsibilities associated with a given *position*, such as that of parent, teacher, manager, physician, ringleader or romantic lover. In this sense, role is something outside the person. *Two*, roles can be seen as a person's *conception* of the part he or she is to play in a given position. In that sense, roles are an aspect of the person. And *three*, one can look at role *behaviour*, that is, the way people actually behave in given positions (and such behaviour presumably relates to their conception of the role). From this point of view one can describe and, possibly, account for individual differences in meeting socially given norms and expectations.

The concept of role, then, refers to socially given expectations in relation to a particular position in a social structure. As such it is perhaps not suited to the analysis of the crowd which, as we have seen, is often thought of as a spontaneously assembled mass of people who do *not* act in accordance with established norms or in a 'normal' social structure. Nevertheless, the concept of role, by stressing that individuals may behave differently when they assume different roles, is useful and not so different from the concept of social identities which people 'switch on' (page 110) according to their perception of the demands of the situation they are in. I shall, therefore, next explore how the notion of social identity has been used in describing and analysing crowds. The question is, is this a concept which can usefully be applied to the explanation of behaviour in crowds as well as in groups?

Social identity and the crowd

Reicher, in the article I have already mentioned, proposes a model of
crowd behaviour which is based on the social identity approach of Tajfel
and Turner (Tajfel, 1978; Turner, 1982). He argues that 'a crowd is a
form of social group in the sense of a set of individuals who perceive themselves as members of a common social category, or, to put it another way,
adopt a common *social* identification' (Reicher, 1984, p. 189). In an
earlier paper he argues that such identity construction does not take place
in a void but in a specific social situation. To quote:

> Consider, once more, a crowd of people watching a fascist rally. To the
> extent that they identify themselves as anti—fascist, they must then clarify
> for themselves what it means to be an anti-fascist in that situation. Suppose
> then that an individual who is seen to fulfil the criteria of being an anti-
> fascist, perhaps by a badge that he wears or by a slogan that he shouts,
> picks up a stone and flings it at the rally. That act, or rather the idea that it
> represents, that of disrupting the fascist rally, can come to be definitional of
> that particular crowd, resulting in a hail of stones, bricks and slogans upon
> the members of the fascist gathering. (Reicher, 1982, pp. 70—1)

In this view, the crowd's behaviour stems from the adoption by the participants of the common social identity of anti-fascist and their behaviour,
in turn, will stem from their knowledge and expectations of how such a
social identity can be or should be expressed in a particular situation.

But perhaps one does not have to explain how a social identity is
adopted in such a situation. Anti-fascists who come to a meeting of fascists
are not there by chance and do, of course, already have a common social
identity through their shared objection to fascism. They rarely become
anti-fascists on the spot. What needs to be explained is how such attitudes
come to be translated into sudden action. One may indeed do so in terms of
the concept of social identity by stating that these attitdes become *salient*
and that the action of one anti-fascist in flinging a stone has shown how
these shared attitudes can be expressed (though those present would not
'normally' throw stones or bricks at anyone).

Other empirical research, however, has shown that the crowd is not
necessarily as like-minded as is sometimes supposed. Thus, Stark and her
colleagues (Stark *et al.*, 1974) found in analysing 1,850 instances of riot
action recorded during the Watts (Los Angeles) riots in 1965 that whereas
some people looted, others burned and that these two types of crowd
actions took place at different times and in different areas. Should we
really consider these different actions, occurring in different locations and
at varying times, to be the expression of a common social identity? This is
perhaps an unanswerable question.

Nevertheless, Reicher (1984) strongly argues for the usefulness of the concept of social identity in explaining the genesis and progress of a recent and relatively small-scale British riot. Certainly, having read his analysis one could not easily fall back on explaining the crowd as a pathological aggregate of people or the behaviour of its members as due to 'primitive' human nature as Le Bon would have it. Scarman, however, in discussing the nature of the 1981 riots in Brixton seems to stress 'primitive human nature' as describing, if not explaining, these events. He states:

> . . . the rioters . . . found a ferocious delight in arson, criminal damage to property, and in violent attacks upon the police, the fire brigade, and the ambulance service. Their ferocity, which made no distinction between the police and the rescue services, is perhaps, the most frightening aspect of a terrifying weekend. (Scarman 1982, p. 77).

Unless we have considerable first hand experience of riots we may not be able to decide whether such riots are due to 'primitive human nature' or the expression of a 'social identity'.

The assembly process

So far we have reviewed some social psychological concepts — deindividuation, roles and social identity — to explore how far they help us in understanding what happens once a crowd is assembled. There is, however, another kind of question (which has particularly interested sociologists) about how people get to the scene of action and through what channels they hear about an event or a disturbance. Remember that we are still looking at protesting, rioting or looting crowds rather than at organized, preplanned assemblies, although disturbances and riots can develop out of organized meetings such as an initially 'peaceful' demonstration against war or racism.

I have suggested in the last section that the anti-fascist rioters may be brought together by a common interest and, one may presume, with prior knowledge of the time and place of the fascist meeting. Their presence, therefore, needs no explanation though their actions perhaps do.

Much more puzzling are sudden outbursts of violence and the escalation of violence which may follow from a relatively minor incident such as an arrest for drunken driving. Empirical studies (see McPhail and Miller, 1973) have shown that large assemblies can be quickly formed in urban ghettos and on college campuses by virtue of the immediate access of large numbers of people in the vicinity. Physical access is also facilitated by major pedestrian and vehicle intersections in the heart of densely populated residential areas and a majority of the 1967 riots in the United States started in or near such areas. It was also found that the majority of these riots originated during the evening or at weekends when large numbers of people were available. It is the 'long hot summers' when everyone is out on the streets at night which may spark off disturbances.

How do people know that something is going on? It is often alleged that news of disturbances or riots on radio or television mobilizes people to come to the area and that later disturbances ('copy-cat' rioting) in other areas are triggered off by such reports. The Kerner Commission (Kerner *et al.*, 1968) in the United States which had been explicitly asked to investigate the role of the mass media in riots found very little evidence in support of this view. Scarman (1982), however, came to the conclusion that the media bore responsibility for the escalation of the disorders (including the looting) in Brixton. Very often, however, it is found that news of rioting travels by word of mouth. Indeed, if riots were caused by information from the mass media, how would one explain their spread in the past? As Field 1982, p. 26) put it, 'when social controls break down, the spread of disorder is dictated by the available means of communication' and he cites Rudé (1967) who points out that eighteenth century food riots spread through France primarily along river valleys. Southgate (1982) in investigating the disturbances in 1981 in Handsworth, Birmingham, found that of those who were actively involved seventy-five per cent said they knew *in advance*. Their responses 'emphasize very strongly the importance of rumour, gossip and the development of an atmosphere of expectation' (Southgate, 1982, p. 25).

Sullivan (1977) and also Lang and Lang (1968) proposed that a 'critical mass' of people is required to spark off a riot. They do not undervalue the importance of precipitating events, for instance, some contact between members of the black community and the police as when police were raiding a club frequented by blacks (this sparked off a riot in Detroit in 1967 and in 1980 the raid by police on a cafe in the St. Paul's area of Bristol led to a riot there). Nevertheless they hold that it is not the grievances people have but the size of a crowd which matters in a riot since 'the larger the crowd, the more easily it can sustain the communication and indications of attitudes and emotions that will influence the behaviour of individuals in the crowd' (Sullivan 1977, p. 52). Lang and Lang (1968) suggest that a 'critical mass' is enough people ready to go into action against control agents, though 'enough' is not further defined. But not all the people on the streets participate in disturbances. Thus Southgate (1982) found that only four per cent of his sample of local residents aged sixteen to thirty-four reported active involvement in rioting but twenty per cent had been on the streets at some time during the troubles (and that figure rose to twenty-five per cent for those aged between sixteen and nineteen). However, it is likely that his interviewees may, for very obvious reasons, have under-reported their own involvement.

The causes of riots

Crowd phenomena are not explicable in terms of social psychological principles alone though the work briefly reviewed here throws some light on the psychological processes at work in the crowd. To fully understand riots and similar outbursts one must investigate the underlying longer-term problems of the areas where rioting occurs, as well as the nature of contemporary events which trigger off particular disturbances.

There is some contemporary as well as historical evidence that riots occur in conditions of *relative deprivation*, that is, when people feel deprived in comparison to others in their society. Riots in the United States occurred in the 1960s mainly in black ghetto areas in which young men grew increasingly frustrated at the extent of unemployment and the social conditions in which they lived compared with the greater affluence amongst other people in their country. American research (McPhail, 1971) showed that the poorest were less likely to riot than more affluent groups (since the latter may, in fact, be more frustrated at their relative lack of opportunity and status than the former). In Britain in 1981 white, black and Asian youngsters rioted, probably, we may suppose, because their expectations of work, training and prospects were not fulfilled in inner city conditions. Unemployment was by far the most common reason given for the disturbances in the locality studied by Southgate (1982) though American studies showed that whilst riots occurred in areas of high unemployment both rioters and non rioters were equally likely to be unemployed. As Field (1982, p. 11) put it: 'It therefore remains possible that unemployment was a causal factor in the riots, although it would achieve its effect through a sense of grievance communicated to the whole ghetto community, rather than through individual unemployed persons becoming more likely to riot.'

If, against the background of deep frustration, one looks at immediate trigger points, one is struck by how frequently both American studies of the 1960s and current British studies show that riots are sparked off by resentment with police action ('over policing'). Recognizing that the immediate trigger may be police activity does not put the sole blame for riots on the police but it does suggest that law enforcement by the police is looked upon with suspicion and anger where there is existing tension and frustration. Furthermore, the police are easily identified targets and they are for rioters both the symbol and reality of the authority of the society which has frustrated them in the first place.

Scarman (1982) therefore recommends that the police establish good relations with all groups in society, But, even more so, we need to learn to understand and to tackle the historical and contemporary roots of the dissatisfaction which erupts into riots — whether such dissatisfactions are due to religious, racial or economic discrimination and inequality. Riots also denote political frustration and a sense that the ordinary political remedies are not available to the rioters. Violent actions by crowds may bring in their wake reassessments and social changes and initiatives. If such rethinking follows on from riots, their effects may prove not to be wholly destructive.

Conclusions to Section IV

Both the public and social scientists are interested in the apparently strange and indeed frightening behaviour individuals engage in in a crowd. Very often 'crowds' are, therefore, treated as something very different from 'groups' and yet, if you think back to the experiments by Milgram (1974) and Zimbardo (1973), you will have instances of dramatic and frightening behaviour of people in *groups* (rather than *crowds*). These group members, too, are behaving in ways which are uncharacteristic of them as individuals. I have, therefore, tried to relate the concepts used in crowd research to the analysis of group phenomena.

One other point: social psychologists have taken the crowd into the laboratory by manipulating such hypothesized characteristics as anonymity or deindividuation. We have seen that they were not wholly successful in doing this. But, even if they had been, does such research capture the flavour of crowd phenomena? Can we indeed generalize from laboratory findings to the wider world (even given that events in the 'wider world' have provided the raw input into the laboratory situation)? There have been many examples in this book of real life events — for instance, conformity, leadership or bystander apathy — being taken successfully into the laboratory and studied under controlled conditions but in the case of crowds laboratory research has not proved equally successful.

SECTION V

Loose Ends and Reflections

In the Introduction I have stated that we will seek to explore the extent to which people's behaviour and subjective experience is under their own control and the extent to which these are determined by outside pressures or, for that matter, as Freud has demonstrated, by unconscious forces over which they have no conscious control. We explored this overarching question by studying behaviour and experience in the group since groups can be shown to have a special importance in human life. We have seen that the extent to which people maintain their autonomy and independence rests on many factors — their goals, the meaning a situation has for them, the pressures on them and their own 'personality', that is, their predispositions, attitudes and past experience. One other factor which enters this equation is knowledge and understanding of the forces which may impinge on us. Such knowledge should enable us to *reflect* on our situation and our actions and help us transcend the pressures which constrain us. Indeed to help create such awareness is an important aim of this book.

Given that the context in which we studied these important issues is the *group*, can we now define this concept with greater precision than we did at the outset?

What is a group?

At the beginning of this book I avoided defining the concept of *group* since a bland definition would be meaningless and a more specific one might prejudge the very issues we were setting out to explore. At the end of the first chapter I still postponed providing *one* definition by referring to groups as an area of study. There were at that point (and still are now) several reasons why it is so difficult to provide one overall and agreed definition of the concept of group.

One, a simple definition will not embrace all the subleties we have come across in this book. For instance, a group can be defined as a collection of individuals who see themselves and/or are seen by others as members of a group. Such a definition is, at the most, a starting point.

Two, the concept of group may encompass anything from small face-to-face groups to large groups such as a nation.

Three, some of the words used in talking about groups, since they denote a psychological relationship or cognitive process or both, can be used about a variety of groups. For instance, a small face-to-face group such as a gang of children can be referred to as a primary group, as a membership group and, if the children treat it as such for certain aspects of their lives, as a reference group. If the street around the corner has produced another gang, the children in each group are likely to think of their own gang as an ingroup and of the other gang as an outgroup. However, apart from the concepts 'primary' and 'face-to-face' which by definition only refer to small groups, all these descriptive or explanatory labels can also be used about large groups such as neighbourhood groups or racial, religious or national groups.

One important thing to understand about groups is that at all times we have multiple group memberships. We can at one and the same time be members of a family, a work group, a religious group, an ethnic group, a fan club, a sports club, of Yorkshire and England and so on. These group memberships need not be mutually exclusive, though I am not suggesting that such multiple memberships are always free from tension.

However, they do not necessarily impinge on our consciousness with equal force. In other words, these group memberships are not necessarily equally salient (that is, psychologically important) to a person at a given point in time or in given circumstances.

Some of the above examples refer to small groups, others belong to the societal level of analysis, but all nevertheless can be referred to as groups — ingroups or outgroups, membership or reference groups.

You may recall that in the Introduction, I stressed the importance of being clear about the level of analysis at which one is operating — the individual, the group or society. It is, in fact, as we have seen throughout our discussions in this book, not always easy to do this, again for several reasons.

Psychologically speaking, a group exists when people think of themselves as members and are affected in their experience or behaviour by their membership. But as my example of multiple group memberships has indicated, some groups are described in terms of societal level concepts or categories such as nations, ethnic groups, the handicapped, the middle class, old age pensioners and so on and others are smaller face-to-face entities.

Furthermore, whilst it is logical and analytically convenient to refer to different levels of analysis, in practice these levels intrude into each other. How you relate to others, say, in a work group, may be influenced by your other group memberships: for instance, in Northern Ireland to be a Catholic may affect relationships with Protestant work mates. In England, whilst religion may not be an issue, race sometimes is.

Throughout this book, we have had many examples of the intrusion of both the individual and the societal levels onto the group level of analysis. To recall just two examples.

Asch who focused on group pressure found great *individual* differences in the reactions of his subjects; later experiments, using his paradigm, showed the influence of *societal* norms, that is, in certain historical periods and in different countries, more or less conformity was in evidence.

Wetherall, in studying the formation and behaviour of 'minimal' groups in New Zealand, found that Maori children differed from their European counterparts in their societal norms of generosity to outsiders and hence behaved differently from the European children in the same experimental situation. This is, of course, what one should expect unless one mistakenly thought that face-to-face group membership *obliterates* everything else — individual differences as much as cultural differences. One lesson to be learnt, therefore, concerns the caution which needs to be used in generalizing from experiments or other kinds of studies carried out in one culture to people in general.

Whilst we may not be able to conclude this book by providing one all inclusive definition for groups, we have been able to be reasonably precise about the nature and psychological implications of the various kinds of groups we have studied and the nature of the influence processes at work among members or between the members of different groups.

There is, of course, not complete agreement on all points. For instance, we have seen that the question of how minorities and majorities within a group affect each other has not been finally resolved. On other issues there is more general agreement. For instance, there is a tendency away from looking on groups as arising from and meeting certain psychological needs to looking on groups as a number of people who perceive and identify themselves as members of the same social category. But, these later developments (which reflect the general movement of psychology and social psychology towards cognitive theories) do not discredit earlier ones. If you are asked why people form groups you can validly reply that (on occasions) they do so because they need each other (to complete a task or for mutual emotional support) *or* you can, equally correctly, reply that (on occasions) they see themselves as a group because they share the same social identity. One reason why these different types of explanation are not mutually exclusive or why they do not contradict each other may be because they refer to different *stages* in the formation and existence of groups. Thus, as Turner (1982) himself agrees, the creation of a social identity (which he sees as the prerequisite for group formation) may depend on such variables as similarity, proximity, the perception of a common fate or shared threat. These are the same variables that earlier theorists held to be important for the formation and cohesion of groups. Hence, the view that some groups are formed because members have the opportunity to meet or have, initially, some common need, interest or goal, or share personal characteritics, and so on, is not invalidated by the view that 'a social group can be usefully conceptualized as a number of individuals who have internalized the same social category membership as a component of their self-concept' (Turner 1982, p. 36). The latter may follow on the former though one can be a member of a group without necessarily identifying to that extent with it.

Sometimes differences are mainly semantic. Thus when Cooley pointed out, at the beginning of this century, that small primary groups are 'natural' and that they, rather than the individual, form the basic human entity he was not so far removed from Tajfel and his colleagues when they showed in recent years in their experiments on 'minimal groups' that groups are formed quite spontaneously so that their members can set their own group off against outsiders. The terminology of their explanations may differ but they describe the same phenomenon. Whether or not we can provide *one* definition for groups for all the phenomena and processes we have described and discussed in this book it has become clear that the study of groups helps us understand our relationships with other people in a wider social context. Nevertheless we are left with some unanswered questions and the psychological interactions between the individual and the group is not always precisely definable or traceable. People vary in their interpretation of a given situation and, furthermore, they usually have several options as to how to react: not everybody succumbs to group pressure and not everybody develops low self-esteem when discriminated against. How we react depends on individual differences, on how far we look on a group as a valid point of reference and on the availability of other meaningful groups which we can join, physically or mentally. People reflect on their situation and problems, they make choices and act independently as well as respond to the pressures and expectations they experience. We are usually keen to think of ourselves as individuals with unique characteristics, in charge of our own decisions (though we seem to be quite willing to describe others in terms of social categories). Many of the descriptive or explanatory concepts used in this book, then, do not precisely define the boundaries between individuals and their groups and societies, but they provide us with ideas and a vocabulary to explore our own situation. For instance, the precise relationships between a person's personal and his or her social identities cannot be predicted but it is interesting to think of people by positing these different identities. Equally, we may not be able to predict who will be regarded as an ingroup member and who will not be so regarded. Indeed, we have seen (in Section III) that people can look on each other as ingroup members in certain settings but not in others, for instance, when working down a mine white workers may feel a sense of solidarity with black fellow workers but this may not be so above ground. I have also shown that the mere presence of people, for instance bystanders at the scene of an emergency where a person needs help, does not of itself lead to the inclusion of the victim in the bystanders' ingroup (as evidenced by the extent to which help is or is not offered) though one might have expected this on the basis of Tajfel's work on 'minimal groups'.

Social psychology and science

In the previous section I wrote that social psychological research and concepts may help us understand ourselves as social beings. But, as I stated in the Introduction, the impetus for much research in social psychology did not necessarily come merely from a desire to understand and explain but arose from immediate social concerns and the hope that knowledge could be generated which would form a basis for intervention and for changing people or their social contexts. This book has demonstrated that, certainly in the study of groups, much social psychological research was in fact sparked off by issues which were seen as 'problematic'. This has certain consequences for social psychology and its practitioners.

There is a tension within social psychology, a tension which was so strongly felt in the 1970s that there was talk of a 'crisis'. This tension exists, in part because of disagreements between those who, from the earliest days, were committed to establishing a socially relevant problem-solving social psychology and those who wished to establish as a first priority a scientific discipline to enhance the status of social psychology without, at that stage, being concerned with the *utility* of their findings. Hence the latter put their efforts into a laboratory-based and theory-oriented hypothesis-testing science. This return to the laboratory was particularly strong in the immediate post-Second World War period during which social psychologists had helped the war effort in various 'applied' ways. Whilst undoubtedly these two views co-exist in social psychology, the chasm between them seems exaggerated. Social psychologists who study a contemporary problem — say, how to resist propaganda or indoctrination or how minority groups achieve influence — can do so by the use of careful scientific methodology and with a view to building a theoretical framework to encompass their findings. Whilst the trigger for research may not have been a scientific hypothesis but a single event (such as the

Kitty Genovese murder) or long standing issues such as intergroup relations in their many guises, research will be undertaken with a view to generate hypotheses and eventually theories. Often many years are spent on developing research into particular topics. We have seen that research traditions have been built in such areas as conformity, minority influence, leadership or bystander apathy and work in these (and other fields) has eventually led to the formulation of theories. Much of the research discussed in this book was based on laboratory research — the preferred method of the scientist — and we have seen that much ingenuity has been used in taking complex social issues, generating hypotheses about the causal connections between various variables and testing these in controlled conditions. The criticism that social psychology is not 'scientific' would not seem appropriate as a general rule. Indeed, the emphasis on laboratory experimentation has called forth other criticism. Experiments have been called artificial and remote from real life. For instance, it has been questioned whether Milgram's experiments 'really' mirror what happened in concentration camps. This seems to me to miss the point. He saw the root of the problem as obedience and he demonstrated that to a large extent it is circumstances and not personality which determine what people do, that is, that most people (and not just those with high scores on the F-scale which denote them as having authoritarian personalities) who find themselves in the situations he created in the laboratory obey the experimenter. Where there is artificiality, it is likely to come about by the *isolation* of variables in the laboratory, whilst in life outside the laboratory they may occur in combination with others. But, this focus on selected variables is also the strength of laboratory experiments and permits causal attributions, other things being equal.

A particular experiment is said to have *internal validity* if the conclusions drawn are properly derived from it. *External or ecological validity* refers to the generalizability of experimental findings to other settings or populations. Many experiments may on their own lack such wider validity, sometimes because the subjects are drawn from restricted samples of the population (frequently only from students). But preliminary findings can be further tested in subsequent laboratory experiments or in field experiments and such findings can be compared to data gained from observations outside the laboratory, from interviews, attitude measurements or surveys. The use of a variety of methods (all of which have some drawbacks and some strengths) may eventually result in ecologically valid findings and insights. Hence whether or not one particular set of experiments has ecological validity is not important so long as it is not unjustifiably claimed that it has such validity. Research almost always leads to further explorations, to more refined hypotheses and eventually also to a theoretical body of knowledge. Nevertheless, because social psychological research has delved into so many aspects of our lives and often pursued a line of investigation without reference to other issues, such theories as we have are often specific to a particular area of investigation. There is a distinct lack of wider ranging theories in social psychology though attempts are being made to relate separate theories to each other. For instance, we have seen that Tajfel's theoretical statements on minimal groups can be related to the theories developed to account for minority influence or that Latané's theorizing about bystander apathy has led him to generalize the notion of 'diffusion of responsibility' and develop his 'social impact theory'. But not all theoretical statements can be related to other theoretical positions, often because the theories offer explanations on different levels of analysis, reflecting different approaches to the exploration of an issue.

In addition to scientific problems, there are also ethical issues which must be faced when carrying out research. Interviews, projective methods or attitudinal tests may all be experienced as intrusive but the question of ethical propriety has been most persistently raised in relation to experiments.

As we have seen, for instance in Milgram's experiments on obedience to authority or in Zimbardo's experimental prison, human participants in experiments can be exposed to situations which they will find disturbing during and after the event. Several points tend to be advanced in mitigation.

One, that, for instance, through simulating conditions of captivity we can learn how not to break down in such conditions or we can even ameliorate life in prisons and hence the cost to subjects is worthwhile.

Two, that, when psychologists carry out disturbing experiments they attempt to 'debrief' their subjects after such experiments (for instance, by telling them that the victim was not really given electric shocks) and hence manage to send them away composed and reassured rather than perturbed by the weakness or callousness of their own characters which they have revealed during the experiments. This seems difficult to achieve though there is some evidence (from a replication of Milgram's studies on obedience to authority which was carried out to evaluate variations in debriefing) to suggest that such procedures may help (Ring, Wallston and Corey, 1970).

Three, that psychologists attempt to gain the subjects' consent to participate in experiments. This in itself may not be quite so in that in many universities students have to put in a certain number of hours as subjects to be given 'credits' for their psychology courses (and this puts pressure on them to agree to participate). But in any case, it is clearly impossible for subjects to give *informed* consent. It would indeed defeat its objective if subjects knew the true purposes of the experiment they are about to participate in and psychologists often have recourse to deception. One cannot say to subjects in advance of the event: 'we want to see under what precise conditions you will succumb to authoritarian pressure' and so on.

What is the solution to such ethical dilemmas? Perhaps ethical issues should not be considered as peripheral but be taken into account right from the first moment of planning research. But the effects on subjects are not always foreseen, for example Milgram did not expect his subjects to become distressed nor did Zimbardo expect such extreme reactions. But, sometimes, the effects on participants are not even mentioned. For instance, the (genuine) passengers on the (genuine) subway carriage in which experiments on bystander apathy were carried out may well have been uneasy after the event about their attitudes or behaviour towards the (apparently) sick or handicapped person who had a fall during the journey.

Strategies for change

Many psychologists and social psychologists do not wish to confine them-selves to an academic role but wish to see their findings translated into solutions for the social ills of their society. They can work towards this aim through publicizing their results, drawing the attention of policy or decision-makers to them and creating an awareness, or a fresh concep-tualization, of an issue. They can also themselves participate in change through working as consultants for programmes of change (for instance by advising on the strategies necessary to gain acceptance and uptake of measures of birthcontrol or by advising on how to improve prison con-ditions or how to reduce prejudice) or they can involve themselves in 'action research', that is, they participate in introducing change and monitor and evaluate the outcomes. An active role in society also of course poses ethical questions. Foremost, I think, one should pause and question whether the advice one offers, or the intervention one is engaged in, is based on sufficient knowledge rather than on findings which may be incomplete and biased by the limited range of questions which have been explored. The second ethical issue focuses on thinking through the likely effects, both planned and unplanned, on the people affected. And third, one must recognize that knowledge can be perverted and used for evil ends. Thus, throughout this book we have seen that group membership can be rewarding and supportive of individuals or it can be used to influence their attitudes or behaviour in ways they would not have chosen freely and as individuals. The *same* knowledge, therefore, can be used to prepare individuals to resist undue pressures or to apply such pressures to them.

Given that ethical concerns should make us cautious in applying our knowledge there are still other barriers to implementing social psycho-logical findings. Put baldly, these arise from the fact that complex social phenomena which we might wish to influence — conformity, racism, authoritarianism, intergroup conflict and so on — rarely have *psychological* solutions. Thus, in order to change people's attitudes and behaviour we may need to change the societal context. I have already referred to this in the conclusions to Section III where I pointed out that to change racial prejudice one needs to implement legal and economic changes so that the context is provided in which better relations can develop or can be fostered.

Let us look at some examples. If you wish to help people to reduce smoking, farmers to adopt new methods of cultivation or fathers to be more involved in the upbringing of their children, then, I would suggest, you need to consider your strategy as it applies to the individual, the group and the societal and cultural context.

Why do people smoke? Some may have an oral fixation in Freudian terms and may be thought to require individual psychoanalytic treatment. Most will have simply formed a habit which they find difficult to break. They may, initially, have started smoking not because it simulated the pleasures of the breast or bottle but because it made them feel adult or 'macho' and was the norm in their social surroundings. Such people and indeed those who smoke for 'deep-seated' reasons may not need psychoanalysis but may respond to behaviour therapy and/or group psychotherapy at a smoking clinic. *But* whichever therapy may have helped them initially, to sustain their newly learned non-smoking behaviour they are likely to need continued support from a special group or from their families or workmates as well as continued information which supports their decision not to smoke. Furthermore, changes in their wider surroundings should also take place so that their individual endeavours are helped by such measures as the prohibition of smoking in offices, libraries, trains and so on. Such prohibitions give a seal of approval to the individual's own struggles and reduce the opportunities of reverting to the old habit of smoking.

How can farmers be helped to improve methods of cultivation? Many studies in developing societies have shown that farmers are quick to learn new methods but slow to implement them. Implementation does not only depend on learning new skills (the individual level) and the approval of others in a similar situation (the group level), it, usually, also requires social system changes — the building of a road from the village to the nearest market town (so that the increased produce can be marketed), the setting-up of a cooperative bank (so that farmers need not sell their crop immediately but can obtain a loan whilst they negotiate a good price) and so on. And, of course, all these things can only happen in a society whose culture emphasizes 'getting on'.

What about our third example, the involvement of fathers in the upbringing of their children? At first sight this seems an entirely personal matter (the individual level) and yet, of course, the father's attitudes and expectations mesh (or need to mesh) with those of his wife and with those of their friends (the group level). Wives and mothers have increasingly moved from their traditional home-bound role into the wider world of work (even when there is no pressing financial need for this). This changed lifestyle has enabled (though some might say forced) fathers to adopt an increasing involvement with their children. 'Society' will need to respond to this new situation by furthering it (through taxation changes, statutory rights to paternity leave, and so on) or by hindering it (by different taxation changes and increased support to mothers who do not take employment outside their homes).

To apply social psychological insights successfully, one needs to make decisions as to the level or levels at which one can most effectively intervene. One may help or influence people directly through information, advice, therapy or by forming groups, or helping people to form groups, as a catalyst for change. Or one may decide to operate on the societal level and to this end join pressure groups or social movements, press for legislative changes or change the wider public's awareness and image of an issue. This book has alerted us to the necessity of considering all these level of analyses and arenas for action.

Finally, I want to return to another point made in the Introduction and that concerns the relevance of social psychology to everyday life. We have seen in this book that much of the 'agenda' for social psychological research is set in the real world. I have also mentioned that early researchers were imbued with optimism and the hope that their work would and could be used to remedy social evils. This early optimism has faded away but should, in my opinion, be rekindled: present-day social psychologists are more sophisticated and competent than their forerunners and they should make the application of their findings a prime objective. But, whether they do or not, people themselves can use social psychological knowledge to make sense of their world. One way in which they can use such knowledge is to be more critical of received truths, platitudes or generalizations. Another way, already mentioned, would be to use the concepts and ideas of social psychology to reflect on their own social world and their experience in it. Lastly, they themselves can use the insights and knowledge gained to intervene in the world and change it. In these ways, social psychological concepts and findings, as did Freud's ideas earlier on, can become part of the culture, part of the shared social representations of our society.

Notes

1. After the Korean War, the Americans defined *indoctrination* as an effort to change a man's viewpoint while he is still a thinking individual by regulating his thoughts and actions (Kinkead 1959, p. 31).
2. Weber (1921) coined the phrase 'charismatic leader' (from the Greek 'charisma' which means divinely inspired power) for those leaders who attract a following because of their strong personalities. Weber points out that charismatic leaders tend to emerge when there is a crisis or a state of distress and uncertainty. Such a leader may, in Freudian terms, represent a common ego-ideal for the group (Freud, 1921/1985)
3. The Japanese consider Harakiri (suicide) as an ultimate expression of autonomy in contrast to Christian religions which condemn suicide (as throwing away God's gift of life). In Britain, in addition to religious disapproval, suicide was a criminal offence until the 1950s, that is, people who attempted but failed to commit suicide could be, and frequently were, charged with a criminal offence.
4. An ethnic group is a collection of people who are considered and, increasingly, who consider themselves to share a common background and present position. They may share racial origins, nationality or cultural traditions such as religion or language. These characteristics do not always go together. We may find that people belong to two ethnic groups simultaneously; for instance, in the Lebanon there are Muslim Arabs and Christian Arabs. Other categorizations may cut across ethnic group membership; for instance, class membership may become more salient to an individual than ethnic group membership (or vice versa).

5. Of course, a distinction can and should perhaps be made between the terms social category and group although the former may become the latter. Once people come to think of themselves in terms of a social category — such as single parent, parents of autistic children, wife of prisoner and so on — then they may seek to join relevant existing groups or create new groups, organizations or social movements to increase the salience of the particular social category to themselves (such as an alumni association) or to gain support for the problems membership of the particular social category presents to the individual.

6. You have earlier (page 35) come across Latané's 'social impact theory' which states that all participants in a group are sources of influence. This view is a generalization from Latané and Darley's findings that bystanders to an emergency are less likely to intervene if others are present than if they are alone. If others are present, the responsibility for intervention is psychologically diffused. Social impact theory suggests that this process is more general and can lead to a diffusion or division of other social forces.

References

ADORNO, T.W., FRENKEL-BRUNSWIK, E., LEVINSON, D.J. and SANFORD, R. (1950). *The authoritarian personality.* New York, Harper and Row.

ALLEN, V.L. (1975). 'Social support for nonconformity', in Berkowitz, L. (ed.) (1975). *Advances in experimental social psychology*, vol. 8, New York, Academic Press.

ALLPORT, G.W. (1954). *The nature of prejudice.* Cambridge, Mass., Addison-Wesley.

AMIR, Y. (1969). 'Contact hypothesis in ethnic relations', *Psychological Bulletin*, 71, pp. 319—42.

ARENDT, H. (1963). *Eichman in Jerusalem.* New York, Viking Press.

ASCH, S.E. (1952). *Effects of group pressure upon modification and distortion of judgements*, in Swanson G.E., Newcomb, T.M. and Hartley, E.L. (eds) (1952). *Readings in social psychology.* New York, Holt, Rinehart and Winston.

ASCH, S.E. (1955). 'Opinions and social pressures', *Sci. American*, 193 pp. 31—55.

BANUAZIZI, A. and MOVAHEDI, S. (1975). 'Interpersonal dynamics in a simulated prison: a methodological analysis', *American Psychologist*, pp. 152—60.

BARTON, W. *et al.*, (1974). *Social psychology: explorations in understanding.* Del Mar, California, CRM Book.

BERGER, P.L. and LUCKMAN, T. (1967). *The social construction of reality.* London, Allen Lane.

BERKOWITZ, L. (1956). 'Personality and group position', *Sociometry*, 19, pp. 210—22.

BETTELHEIM, B. (1943). 'Individual and mass behaviour in extreme situations', *Journal of Abnormal and Social Psychology*, xxxviii, pp. 417—52.

BILLIG, M. (1979). 'Professor Eysenck's political psychology', *Patterns of Prejudice*, 13 (5), pp. 8—16.

BILLIG, M. (1982). *Ideology and social psychology.* Oxford, Blackwell.

BILLIG, M. and TAJFEL, H. (1973). 'Similarity and categorization in intergroup behaviour', *European J. Social Psychology*, 3, 1, pp. 27—53.

BION, W.R. (1961). *Experiences in groups.* London, Macmillan.

BRAY, R.M. *et al.*, (1982). 'Social influence by group members with minority opinions: a comparison of Hollander and Moscovici', *Journal of Personality and Social Psychology*, 43, 1, pp. 78—88.

BROWN, R.J. and TURNER, J.C. (1981). 'Interpersonal and intergroup behaviour' in Turner, J.C. and Giles, H. (eds) (1981). *Intergroup behaviour.* Oxford, Blackwell.

BYRNE, D. (1971). *The attraction paradigm.* New York, Academic Press.

CAIRNS, E. (1982). 'Intergroup conflict in Northern Ireland', in Tajfel, H. (ed.) (1982). *Social Identity and Intergroup Relations*. Cambridge, Cambridge University Press.

CARTWRIGHT, D. (1979). 'Contemporary social psychology in historical perspective', *Social Psychology Quarterly*, 42, 1, pp. 82—93.

CLARK, K.B. and CLARK, M.P. (1947) 'Racial identification and preference in Negro children' in Maccoby, E.E., Newcomb, T.M. and Hartley, E.L. (eds.) (1958) Readings in Social Psychology New York Holt, Rinehart and Winston.

COCH, L. and FRENCH, J.R.P. (1948). 'Overcoming resistance to change,' *Hum. Rel. I.*, pp. 512—32.

COOLEY, C.H. (1902). *Human nature and the social order*. New York, Shocken (1964).

COSER, L.A. (1967). *Continuities in the study of social conflict*. New York, Free Press.

DAVIS, J.H. (1969). *Group performance*. Reading, Mass., Addison-Wesley.

DAVIS, J.H. and HORNSETH, J.P. (1967). 'Discussion patterns and world problems', *Sociometry*, 30, pp. 91—103.

DEUTSCH, M. and COLLINS, M.E. (1951). *Interracial housing: a psychological evaluation of a social experiment*. Minneapolis, University of Minnesota Press.

DEUTSCH, M. and GERARD, H. (1955). 'A study of normative and informational social influences on individual judgement', 'J. Abnorm. and Soc. Psychol., 51, pp. 629—36.

DIENER, E. (1980). 'Deindividuation: the absence of self-awareness and self-regulation in group members', in Paulus, P.B. (ed.) *Psychology of group influence*. Hillsdale, New Jersey, Lawrence Erlbaum Associates.

DURKHEIM, E. (1897). *Rules of sociological method*. New York, Free Press (1950).

DWYER, P.M. (1979). 'An enquiry into the psychological dimensions of cult suicide', *Suicide and life threatening behaviour*, 9, (2), pp. 120—7.

EDUCATION FOR ALL. (1985). *Report of the committee of enquiry into the education of children from ethnic minority groups*. Cmnd 9453, London, Stationary Office.

ELLUL, J. (1965). *Propaganda: the formation of men's attitudes*. New York, Vintage Books.

EYSENCK, H.J. (1954). *The psychology of politics*. London, Routledge and Kegan Paul.

FESTINGER, L. (1953). *An analysis of compliant behaviour* in Sherif, M. and Wilson, M.O. (eds) (1953). *Group relations at the crossroads* New York, Harper.

FESTINGER, L. (1954). 'A theory of social comparison processes', *Human Relations*, 7, pp. 117—40.

FESTINGER, L. (1957). *A theory of cognitive dissonance*. Evanston, Illinois, Row, Paterson.

FESTINGER, L. and CARLSMITH, J.M. (1959). 'Cognitive consequences of forced compliance', *Journal of Abnormal and Social Psychology*, 58, pp. 203—10.

FESTINGER, L., PEPITONE, A. and NEWCOMB, T. (1952). 'Some consequences of dein-dividuation in a group', *Journal of Abnormal and Social Psychology*, 47, pp. 382—9.

FIEDLER, F.E. (1965). 'Engineer the job to fit the manager', *Harvard Business* Review, pp. 115—22.

FIEDLER, F.E. (1967). *A theory of leadership effectiveness*. New York, McGraw Hill.

FIEDLER, F.E. (1968). 'Personality and situational determinants of leadership effectiveness', in Cartwright, D. and Zander, A. (eds) *Group dynamics*. New York, Harper and Row.

FIEDLER, F.E. (1971). 'Validation and extension of the contingency model of leadership effective-ness: a review of empirical findings', *Psychology Bulletin*, 76, pp. 128—48.

FIEDLER, F.E. (1972). 'Personality motivational systems and the behaviour of high and low LPC', *Human Relations*, 25, pp. 391—412.

FIELD, S. (1982). 'Urban disorders in Britain and America: a review of research', in Field, S. and Southgate, P. (1982). *Public disorder, a Home Office Research and Planning Unit Report* London. HMSO.

FRANKS, (LORD) (1983). *Falkland Islands review, report of a committee of Privy Councillors CMND 8787*. London, HMSO.

FREUD, S. (1921). *Group psychology and the analysis of the ego. Standard Edition*, vol. 18, London, Hogarth Press (1955). Reprinted in Volume 12 of the Pelican Freud Library (1985), Harmondsworth, Penguin Books.

FROMM, E. (1941). *Escape from freedom*. New York, Farrar and Rhinehart.

GANS, H.J. (1972). *People and plans: essays on urban problems and solutions*. Harmondsworth, Penguin.

GOFFMAN, E. (1968). *Asylums*. Harmondsworth, Penguin.

GOFFMAN, E. (1971). *The presentation of self in everyday life*. Harmondsworth, Penguin.

GRAF, R.G. and RIDDELL, J.C. (1972). 'Helping behaviour as a function of interpersonal perception', *J. Social Psychol.*, 86, pp. 227—31.

HEARST, CAMPBELL, P. (1983). *Every secret thing*. London, Arrow Books.

HEBB, D.O. *et al*. (1952). 'The effects of isolation upon attitudes, motivation and thought', *Fourth Symposium, Military Medicine I.*, Defence Research Board, Canada.

HEWSON, D. (1982). 'Fireproof uniforms anger blacks', *The Times*, April 22nd, London.

HOLLANDER, E.P. (1958). 'Conformity, status and idiosyncrasy credit', *Psychology Review*, 65, pp. 117—27.

HOLLANDER, E.P. and JULIAN, J.W. (1970). 'Studies in leader legitimacy, influence and innovation' in Berkowitz, L. (ed.) *Advances in experimental social psychology*, 5, New York, Academic Press.

HOMANS, G.C. (1961). *Social behaviour: its elementary forms*. New York, Harcourt Brace Jovanovich.

HOVLAND, C.I. and JANIS, I.L. (1959). *Personality and persuasibility*. New Haven, Yale University Press.

HOVLAND, C.I., JANIS, I.L. and KELLY, H.H. (1953). *Communication and persuasion*. New Haven, Conn., Yale University Press.

HRABA, J. and GRANT, C. (1970). 'Black is beautiful: a re-examination of racial identification and preference'. *Journal of Personality and Social Psychology*, 16, pp. 398—402.

HYMAN, H.H. (1942). *The psychology of status Archs. Psychology*, No. 269, New York, Columbia University.

JAHODA, M, (1959). 'Conformity and independence — a psychological analysis' *Human Relations*, 12, pp. 99—120.

JAHODA, M. (1982). 'Individual and group', in Pines, M. and Rafaelsen, L. (eds) *The individual and the group*. vol. I: Theory, New York, Plenum Press.

JANIS, I.L. (1982). *Victims of group think: a psychological study of foreign policy decisions and fiascos*. Boston, Mass., Houghton, Mifflin, 2nd edition.

JENKINS, B.M. (1975). *Hostages and their captors: friends and lovers* Santa Monica, California, Rand.

KATZ, E. (1957). 'The two-step flow of communication'. *Public Opinion Quarterly*, vol. 21, pp. 61—78.

KELMAN, H.C. (1958). 'Compliance, identification and internalization: three processes of attitude change, *Journal of Conflict Resolution*, 2, pp. 51—60.

KERNER, O. *et al*. (1968). *Report of the national advisory commission on civil disorders*, Washington, US Government Printing Office.

KINKEAD, E. (1959). *Why they collaborated*. London, Longman.

LAING, R.D. (1970). *The divided self*. Harmondsworth, Penguin Books.

LANG, K. and LANG, G.E. (1968). 'Racial disturbances as collective protest', *American Behavioural Scientist*, 11, pp. 11—13.

LA PIERE, R.T. (1934). 'Attitudes versus actions', Social Forces, 13, pp. 230—7.

LARSEN, K.S. (1974). 'Conformity in the Asch experiment', *Journal of Social Psychology*, 94, pp. 303—4.

LARSEN, K.S. (1982). 'Cultural conditions and conformity: the Asch effect', *Bulletin of the British Psychological Society*, 35, p. 347.

LARSEN, K.S., TRIPLETT, J.S., BRANT, W.D. and LANGENBERG, D. (1979). 'Collaborator status, subject characteristics and conformity in the Asch paradigm', in *Journal of Social Psychology*, 108, pp. 259—63.

LATANÉ, B, and DARLEY, J.M. (1968). 'Group inhibition of bystander intervention in emergencies', *Journal of Personality and Social Psychology*, 10, pp. 215—21.

LATANÉ, B. and RODIN, J. (1969). 'A lady in distress: inhibiting effects of friends and strangers on bystander intervention', *Journal of Exp. Social Psychology*, 5, pp. 189—202.

LATANÉ, B. and DARLEY, J.M. (1970). *The unresponsive bystander: why does he not help?*, New York, Appleton-Century-Crofts.

LATANÉ, B. and DARLEY, J.M. (1976). *Help in a crisis: bystander response to an emergency*, Morristown, New Jersey, General Learning Press.

LATANÉ, B. and NIDA, S. (1980). 'Social impact theory and group influence: a social engineering perspective in Paulus, P.B. (ed.). *Psychology of group influence*. Hillsdale, New Jersey, Erlbaum.
LATANÉ, B. and WOLF, S. (1981). 'The social impact of majorities and minorities' Psychological Review, Vol. 88, 5 pp. 438—53.
LAZARSFELD, P.F., BERELSON, B. and GAUDET, H. (1948). *The people's choice: how the voter makes up his mind in a presidential campaign*. New York, Columbia University Press.
LEAVITT, J.J. (1951). 'Some effects of certain communication patterns on group performance', *Journal of Abnormal Social Psychology*, 46, pp. 38—50.
LE BON, G. (1895). *The crowd: a study of the popular mind*. London, Ernest Benn (1952).
LEVY, L. (1960). 'Studies in conformity behaviour: a methodological note', *Journal of Psychology*, 50, pp. 39—41.
LEWIN, K. (1947). 'Group decision and social change', in Newcomb, T.M. and Hartley, E.L. (eds)(1947). *Readings in social psychology*. New York, Holt, Rinehart and Winston.
LEWIN, K. (1948). *Resolving social conflicts: selected papers on group dynamics*. New York, Harper and Brothers.
LEWIN, K., LIPPITT, R. and WHITE, R. (1939). 'Patterns of aggressive behaviour in experimentally created "social climates" ', *Journal of Social Psychology*, 10, pp. 271—99.
LIFTON, R.J. (1957). 'Thought reform of Chinese intellectuals', *Journal of* Social Issues, 13, pp. 5—20.
LIFTON, R.J. (1961). *Thought reform and the psychology of totalism: a study of 'brainwashing' in China*. London, Gollancz.
LUCHINS, A.S. and LUCHINS, E.H. (1955). 'On conformity with true and false communications', *Journal of Social Psychology*, 42, pp. 283—303.
MAASS, A., CLARK, R.D. III and HABERKORN, G. (1982). 'The effects of differential ascribed category membership and norm on minority influence', *European Journal of Social Psychology*, 12, pp. 89—104.
MAASS, A. and CLARK, R.D. (1984). 'Hidden impact of minorities: fifteen years of minority influence research', *Psychological Bulletin*, 95, 3, pp. 428—50.
MCPHAIL, C. (1971). 'Civil disorder participation: a critical examination of recent research', *American Sociol. Review*, 36, pp. 1058—71.
MCPHAIL, C. and MILLER, D. (1973). 'The assembly process: a theoretical and empirical examination', *American Sociol. Review*, 38, pp. 721—35.
MENZEL, H. and KATZ, E. (1955). 'Social relations and innovation in the medical profession: the epidemiology of a new drug', *Public Opinion Quarterly*, vol. 19, pp. 337—52.
MILGRAM, S. (1961). 'Nationality and conformity', *Scientific American*, vol. 205, 6, pp. 45—51.
MILGRAM, S. (1974). *Obedience to authority*. London, Tavistock.
MILGRAM, S. and TOCH, H. (1969). 'Collective behaviour: crowds and social movements', in Lindzey, G. and Aronson, E. (eds) (1969), *The handbook of social psychology*, vol. IV, (2nd edition).
MILNER, D. (1984). 'The development of ethnic attitudes', in Tajfel, H. (ed.) (1984). *The social dimension*. vol. I, Cambridge, Cambridge University Press.
MINARD, R.D. (1952). 'Race relationships in the Pocahontas coal fields', *Journal of Social Issues*, 25, pp. 29—44.
MINISTRY OF DEFENCE. (1955). *Treatment of British prisoners of war in Korea*. London, HMSO.
MOSCOVICI, S. (1961). *La Psychoanalyse, son image et son public* (2nd edn 1976) Paris, Presses Universitaires de France.
MOSCOVICI, S. (1976). *Social influence and social change*. London, Academic Press.
MOSCOVICI, S. (1980). 'Towards a theory of conversion behaviour', in Berkowitz, L. (ed.) *Advances in experimental social psychology*, vol. 13, New York, Academic Press.
MOSCOVICI, S. and FAUCHEUX, X. (1972). 'Social influence, conformity bias and the study of active minorities', in Berkowitz, L. (ed.) *Advances in experimental social psychology*, vol. 6, New York, Academic Press.
MOSCOVICI, S., LAGE, E. and NAFFRECHOUX, M. (1969). 'Influence of a consistent minority on the response of a majority in a color perception task', *Sociometry*, 32, pp. 365—80.
MUGNY, G. (1975). 'Negotiations, image of the other and the process of minority influence', *European Journal of Social Psychology*, 5, pp. 209—29.

MUGNY, G. (1982), *The power of minorities*. London, Academic Press.

MUGNY, G., KAISER, C., PAPASTAMOU, S. and PÉREZ, J.A. (1984). 'Intergroup relations, identification and social influence', *British Journal of Social Psychology*, 23, pp. 317—22.

MURPHY, J., JOHN, M. and BROWN, H. (eds) (1984) *Dialogues and debates in social psychology*. London, Erlbaum/Open University Press.

NAIPAUL, S. (1981). *Black and white*. London, Sphere Books.

NEMETH, C.J. and WACHTLER, J. (1983). 'Creative problem solving as a result of majority versus minority influence', *European Journal of Social Psychology*, 13, pp. 45—55.

NEWCOMB, T.M. (1952). Attitude development as a function of reference groups: the Bennington study', in Swanson, G.E. *et al.)* (1952). (eds) *Readings in Social Psychology*. New York, Holt, Rinehart and Winston.

NEWCOMB, T.M., KOEING, K.E., FLACKS, R. and WARWICK, D.P. (1967). *Persistence and change: Bennington college and its students after 25 years*. New York, Wiley.

NEWMAN, O. (1972). *Defensible space*. New York, Macmillan.

NICHOLSON, N., COLE, S.G. and ROCKLIN, T. (1985). 'Conformity in the Asch situation: a comparison between contemporary British and US university students', *British Journal of Social Psychology*, 24, pp. 59—63.

NOELLE-NEUMANN, E. (1984). *The spiral of silence: public opinion — our social skin*. Chicago, The University of Chicago Press.

ORNE, M.T. (1962). 'On the social psychology of the psychological experiment', *American Psychologist*. 17, 11, pp. 776—83.

OSMOND, H. (1957). 'Function as the basis of psychiatric ward design', in Proshansky, H.M. *et al*. (1970). *Environmental psychology: man and his physical setting*. New York, Holt, Rinehart and Winston.

PAICHELER, G. (1979). 'On the comparability of experimental results', *European Journal of Social Psychology*, 9, pp. 227—8.

PELZ, E.B. (1958. 'Some factors in "group decision" ', in Maccoby, E.E., Newcomb, T.M. and Hartley, E.L. (eds) (1958). *Readings in social psychology*, (3rd edn), New York, Holt, Rinehart and Winston.

PERRIN, S. and SPENCER, C. (1981). 'Independence or conformity in the Asch experiment as a reflection of cultural and situational factors', *Brit J. of Social Psychology*, 20, pp. 205—9.

PETTIGREW, T.F. (1958). 'Personality and socio-cultural factors in intergroup attitudes: a cross-national camparison', *J. Conflict Resolution*, 2, pp. 29—42.

PETTIGREW, T.F. (1964). *A profile of the American negro*. Princeton, Van Nostrand.

PETTIGREW, T.F. (1971). *Racially separate or together*? New York, McGraw Hill.

PILIAVIN, I.M., RODIN, J. and PILLIAVIN, J.A. (1969). 'Good samaritanism: an underground phenomenon?, *J. of Pers. and Soc. Psychol.*, 13, pp. 289—99.

PILIAVIN, I.M., PILIAVIN, J.A. and RODIN, S. (1975). 'Costs, diffusion and the stigmatised victim, J. Pers and Soc. Psychol., 32, pp. 429—38.

PILIAVIN, J.A. and PILIAVIN, I.M. (1972). 'Effect of blood on reactions to a victim', *Journal of Personality and Social Psychology*, 23, pp. 353—62.

PILIAVIN, J.A. *et al.* (1981). *Emergency intervention*. New York, Academic Press.

REICHER, S.D. (1982). The determinants of collective behaviour', in Tajfel, H. (ed.) (1982). op. cit.

REICHER, S.D. (1984). 'St. Paul's: A study in the limits of crowd behaviour', in Murphy, John and Brown (1984), op. cit.

RILEY, J.W. Jr. and RILEY M.W. (1959). 'Mass communication and the social system', in Merton, R.K., Broom, L. and Cottrell, L.S. Jr. (eds) (1959). *Sociology today: problems and prospects*, vol. II, pp. 537—87), New York, Basic Books.

RING, K., WALLSTON, K. and COREY, M. (1970). 'Role of debriefing as a factor affecting subjective reaction to a Milgram type obedience experiment: an ethical enquiry', *Representative research in social psychology*, 1 (1), pp. 67—88.

ROETHLISBERGER, F.J. and DICKSON, W.J. (1939). *Management and the worker*. Cambridge, Mass., Harvard University Press.

ROGERS, E.M. (1962). *Diffusion of innovations*. New York, The Free Press.

ROKEACH, M. (1960). *The open and closed mind*. New York, Basic Books.

ROKEACH, M. (1968). *Beliefs, attitudes and values* San Francisco, Jossey-Bass.
ROSENTHAL, R. (1966). *Experimenter effects in behavioural research*. New York, Appleton-Century-Crofts.
RUDÉ, G. (1967). *The crowd in history*. New York, Wiley.
SAVIN, H.B. (1973). 'Professors and psychological researchers: conflicting values in conflicting roles', *Cognition*, 2 (1), pp. 147—9.
SAYLES, S.M. (1966). 'Supervisory style and productivity: review and theory', *Personnel psychology*, 19, 3, pp. 275—86.
SCARMAN (The Right Honourable Lord Scarman)(1981). The Brixton disorders 10—12 April, 1981. Cmnd. no. 8427, London, HMSO. (republished by Penguin Books 1982).
SCHEIN, E.H. (1956). 'The Chinese indoctrination program for prisoners of war', *Psychiatry*, 19, pp. 149—73.
SCHEIN, E.H. (1957). 'Reaction patterns to severe chronic stress in American Army prisoners of war', *Journal of Social Issues*, 13, pp. 21—30.
SCHWARTZ, S.H. and GOTTLIEB, A. (1976). 'Bystander reaction to a violent theft: crime in Jerusalem', *Journal of Personality and Social Psychology*, 34, pp. 1181—99.
SECORD, P.F. and BACKMAN, C.W. (1964). *Social psychology*. New York, McGraw-Hill.
SHERIF, M. (1936). *The psychology of social norms*. New York, Harper and Row.
SHERIF, M. and SHERIF, C.W. (1953). *Groups in harmony and tension*. New York, Harper Brothers.
SHERIF, M., WHITE, B.J. and HARVEY, O.J. (1955). *Experimental study of positive and negative intergroup attitudes between experimentally produced groups: robbers cave study*. Norman. University of Oklahoma.
SHERIF, M., HARVEY, O.J., WHITE, B.J., HOOD, W.R. and SHERIF, C. (1961). *Intergroup cooperation and competition: the robbers cave experiment*, Norman, University of Oklahoma.
SHERIF, M. and SHERIF, C. (1969). *Social Psychology*. New York, Harper and Row.
SHILS, E.A. (1954). 'Authoritarianism: "right" and "left", in Christie, R. and Jahoda, M. (eds) *Studies in the scope and method of 'the authoritarian personality'*. Glencoe, Illinois, Free Press.
SIMPSON, M.A. (1976). 'Brought in dead', *Omega: Journal on Death and Dying*, 7, pp. 243—8.
SINGER, J.E., BRUSH, C.A. and LUBLIN, S.C. (1965). 'Some aspects of deindividuation: identification and conformity', *J. Exp. Soc. Psychol.*, 1, pp. 356—78.
SISTRUNK, F. and MCDAVID, J.W. (1971). 'Sex variables in conformity behaviour', *Journal of Personality and Social Psychology*, 17, pp. 200—7.
SMITH, P.B. (1984). 'The effectiveness of Japanese styles of management: a review and critique', *Journal of Occupational Psychology*, 57, pp. 121—36.
SORRELL, W.E. (1978). 'Cults and cult suicide', *International Journal of Group Tensions*, 8, pp. 96—105.
SOUTHGATE, P. (1982). 'The disturbances of July 1981 in Handsworth, Birmingham: a survey of the views and experiences of male residents', in Field, S. and Southgate, P. (1982). *Public disorder, a Home Office Research and Planning Unit Report*. London, HMSO.
STARK, M.J.A. *et al.* (1974). 'Some empirical patterns in a riot process', *American Soc. Review*, 39, pp. 865—76.
SUDNOW, D. (1973). 'Dead on arrival', *Interaction*, November 1973, pp. 23—31.
SULLIVAN, T.J. (1977). 'The "critical mass" in crowd behaviour: crowd size, contagion and the evolution of riots', *Humboldt J. Soc. Relat.*, 4, 2, pp. 46—59.
TAJFEL, H. (1978). *Differentiation between social groups: studies in the social psychology of inter-group relations*. London, Academic Press.
TAJFEL, H. (ed.) (1982). *Social identity and intergroup relations*, London/Paris, Cambridge University Press/Editions de la Maison des Sciences de L'Homme.
TAJFEL, H., BILLIG, M.G. and BUNDY, R.P. (1971). 'Social categorization and intergroup behaviour', *European Journal of Social Psychology*, vol. 1, no. 2, pp. 149—78.
TAJFEL, H. and TURNER, J. (1979). 'An integrative theory of intergroup conflict', in Austin, G.W. and Worchel, S. (eds) (1979). *The social psychology of intergroup relations*. Monterey, California, Brooks/Cole.
THOMAS, W.I. and ZNANIECKI, F. (1918). The Polish Peasant in Europe and America (5 volumes) Boston, Richard Badger.

TRIST, E.L., HIGGINS, G.W., MURRAY, H. and POLLOCK, A.B. (1963). *Organizational choice*. London, Tavistock.

TURNER, J.C. (1982). 'Towards a cognitive redefinition of the social group', in Tajfel, H. (ed.) (1982) op. cit.

TYERMAN, A. and SPENCER, C. (1983). 'A critical test of the Sherifs' robber's cave experiments: intergroup competition and cooperation between groups of well-acquainted individuals', *Small Group Behaviour*. 14, 4, pp. 515—31.

UNGERLEIDER, J.T. and WELLISCH, D.K. (1979). 'Coercive persuasion (brainwashing), Religious cults, and deprogramming', *American Journal of Psychiatry*, 136: 3, pp. 279—82.

WATSON, P. (1980). *War on the mind: the military uses and abuses of psychology*. Harmondsworth, Penguin Books.

WEBER, M. (1921). *The sociology of charismatic authority*, in Gerth, H.H. and Mills, C.W. (translaters and editors): *From Max Weber: essays in sociology*. London, Oxford University Press.

WETHERALL, M. (1982). 'Cross-cultural studies of minimal groups: implications for the social identity theory of intergroup relations', in Tajfel, H. (ed.)(1982) op. cit.

WOHLSTETTER, R.(1962). *Pearl Harbour: warning and decision*. Stamford, Stamford University Press.

WOODWARD, J. (1965). *Industrial organization: theory and practice*. London, Oxford University Press.

YEE, M.S. and LAYTON, T.N. (1981).*In my father's house: the story of the Layton family and the Reverend Jim Jones*. New York, Holt, Rinehart and Winston.

ZIMBARDO, P.G. (1969). *The human choice: individuation, reason, and order versus deindividuation, impulse, and chaos*, in Arnold, W.J. and Levine, D. (eds)*Nebraska symposium on motivation* (1969), Lincoln, University of Nebraska Press.

ZIMBARDO, P.G., BANKS, W.C., CRAIG, H. and JAFFE, D. (1973). 'A pirandellian prison: the mind is a formidable jailer', *New York Times Magazine*, 8 April 1973, pp. 38—60.

ZIMBARDO, P.G. (1973). 'On the ethics of intervention in human psychological research with special reference to the Stanford Prison experiment', *Cognition*, 2, (2) pp. 243—55.

Author Index

Subject Index